Practical Guide to the Operational Use of the M79 Grenade Launcher

By Erik Lawrence

Copyright ©2014 Erik Lawrence

Erik Lawrence
www.vig-sec.com   erik@vig-sec.com

Printed and bound in the United States of America

First printing 2008
Second Printing 2014

ISBN-10: 1-941998-11-9
ISBN-13: 978-1-941998-11-3
EBOOK – ISBN-13: 978-1-941998-30-4

LCCN: Not yet assigned

ATTENTION US MILITARY UNITS, US GOVERNMENT AGENCIES AND PROFESSIONAL ORGANIZATIONS: Quantity discounts are available on bulk purchases of this book. Special books or book excerpts can also be created to fit specific needs. For information, please contact:

Erik Lawrence
www.vig-sec.com   erik@vig-sec.com

SAFETY NOTICE
Before starting an inspection, ensure the weapon is cleared. Do not manipulate the trigger system until the weapon has been cleared of all ammunition. Inspect the chamber to ensure that it is empty and no ammunition is present. Keep the weapon oriented in a safe direction when loading and handling.

AMMUNITION NOTICE - These weapons fire multiple types of grenades and they must come from trusted sources; never fire captured grenades. Know the capabilities and limitation of each type of grenade. The 40 mm grenades used in the M79 (40x46mm) are not the same as in the Mk 19 grenade launcher (40x53mm), which are fired at a higher velocity. Firing the incorrect ammunition will damage the weapon and possibly injure the operator/assistant operator. After approximately 15 meters of flight, the grenade is armed.

Training should be received from knowledgeable and experienced operators on this particular weapons system. Vigilant Security Services, LCC Training provides this training and continually perfects its instruction with up-to-date information from actual use.

www.vig-sec.com

PREFACE

This manual is intended to be a reference for those involved in the use, maintenance and instruction of the featured firearm. My aim in writing these manuals is to set the record straight and dispel many of the false assumptions related to the different firearms. The early sections of the manual contain background material on the featured firearm which allows the user to gain the basic building blocks for further education. The firearms featured in these manuals have been used for decades by our allies and enemies, and will be for the foreseeable future, so why are we not experts with them? If I am fighting with the firearm or providing instruction on a firearm, I want to use and know their system better than they do.

The rationale for writing these manuals comes from the fact that there are not libraries of easily accessible references to use in developing your own training system for these firearms. Many of the old military field manuals are decades old and were incorrectly translated by someone who had no idea what the firearm could do, let alone basic firearm knowledge. We started from the ground up and developed the manuals to provide instruction in progressive steps that could be easily grasped and continually referred back to. A good grounding in the basics of firearms, safety, and instruction allows the user to use these manuals to their maximum value. A competent user will find little difficulty in interpreting and applying the information in the manual to their own training program.

The guide goes through the most fundamental parts of the firearm in detail and more advanced techniques are not covered as extensively. With this in mind the user can use these principles and adapt it as needed to their required level of instruction. The emphasis of this guide is in acquiring familiarity with the fundamentals of all firearms and learned competence rather than becoming a firearms guru.

Many of the points in these guides were developed from scratch in theatres of conflict and are continually improved and updated for each edition. I have continually used vetted points from users and professionals in the guides to continually update them to the best known practices for each particular firearm. If it is valid and relevant we will include it in the next edition.

Please note that this guide assumes some familiarity with the basic concepts in firearm safety, gun handling skills, common sense and an ability to process new information. Readers should have knowledge of the difference in calibers, countries of origin, and the knowledge of the priority of the skills needed for development.

I hope you find this work useful and remember that a manual does not replace proper training and hands on experience. Please email comments to erik@vig-sec.com, particularly if you find any errors or glaring omissions.

Erik Lawrence

Table of Contents

M79

Grenade Launcher

Section 1

Introduction

The objective of this manual is to allow the reader to be able to use the M79 Grenade Launcher competently. The manual will give the reader background/specifications of the weapon; instructions on its operation, disassembly and assembly; proper firing procedure; and malfunction/misfire procedures. Operator-level maintenance will also be detailed to allow the reader to understand and become competent in the use and maintenance of the M79 Grenade Launcher.

Description

Figure 1-1 M79 Grenade Launcher

The M79 Grenade Launcher is a single-shot, break-open, breech-loading, shoulder-fired weapon (Figure 1-1). It consists of a receiver group, fore-end assembly, barrel group, sight assembly, stock assembly, and sling. A rubber recoil pad is attached to the butt of the stock to absorb some of the recoil. The M79 Grenade Launcher was designed to fire a 40mm grenade more accurately than when fired from a rifle grenade launcher.

he M79 was a standard single-shot, squad-support weapon that made its initial appearance with American troops during the Vietnam War. The system could lob a grenade projectile several hundred meters away and stop light-armored vehicles or flush out enemy elements from dug-in or elevated positions.

The M79 has been in service with the US Army and Marine Corps since 1961, and it is in service with many other militaries. It is currently being superseded in US service by the M203.

The secret to the success of the M79 was a high-low pressure system that allowed the propellant to develop a relatively high pressure in a high-pressure chamber before venting gases into a low-pressure chamber in the grenade cartridge case.

The M79 was the first weapon to come into service which was specifically designed to fire spin-stabilized grenades. It is a light weapon with acceptable recoil and an adequate range. A trained man can fire a grenade with great precision up to 150 m range.

The M79 was designed to launch a variety of ammunition types, including HE, flechette, buckshot, smoke, and non-lethal rounds. The system itself was very simplistic featuring a breech-loading component with static iron sights (the user would load the weapon by folding the barrel portion forward, similar to what is done to load some shotgun types). A folding "ladder" sight was also prominently integrated for elevated-range firing. The single-shot capability proved to be a major drawback as the user was unable to keep up any well-respected rate of fire on enemy positions for suppression purposes.

The characteristics of the M79 grenade Launcher:

A. Country of Origin: USA

B. Military Designation: M79

C. Weight-
   a. Unloaded   6 pounds (2.72 kg)
   b. Loaded   6.5 pounds (2.95 kg)
D. Length-
   a. Launcher (overall)   29 inches (73.7 cm)
   b. Barrel group   15 inches (38.1 cm)
   c. Barrel only   14 inches (35.6 cm)

E. Cartridge Type: 40x46mm low-velocity grenade cartridge

F. Muzzle Velocity: 76 meters per second (250 fps)

G. Type of Feed: Single-shot

H. Action: Breech-loaded, break-open

I. Chamber Pressure: 17,685 kilopascals (3,000 PSI)

J. Sights:
   a. Front- Blade-type
   b. Folding leaf-type, adjustable

K. Maximum Range: 400 meters (1,312 feet)

L. Maximum Effective Range:
    a. Area target-   350 meters (1,148 feet)
    b. Point target-   150 meters (492 feet)

M. Minimum Safe Firing Range:
    a. Training-   130 meters (426 feet)
    b. Combat-   31 meters (102 feet)

Background

Grenade launchers were delivered to the US Army. They were designed as a close support weapon for the infantry in order to bridge the gap in range between hand-thrown grenades and mortars (between 50 and 300 meters). This unique ability gave the squad a very lethal, integral indirect-fire weapon.

The M79 was a product of the failure of Project NIBLICK to create an envisioned multi-shot 40mm system for which the cartridge had originally been designed. In many respects a crude system, the M79 nevertheless provided an excellent force multiplier until the arrival of the first generation of under barrel grenade launchers (UGLs), the XM148 and the XM203. Commonly known as the "Thump-Gun," "Thumper," or "Blooper" in US service, it is also known to some Australian units as the "Wombat Gun." It closely resembles a large bore, break-action, sawn-off shotgun, and can fire a wide variety of 40mm rounds, including explosive, anti-personnel, smoke, buckshot, flechette, and incendiary. During the 1960s and '70s, the US experimented with many types of grenade launchers attached to rifles, which allowed the grenadier to also function as a rifleman.

These weapons were developed because the M79's greatest drawback proved to be its single-shot-only capability. This left the user totally unable to keep up a constant volume of fire during a firefight, and often grenadiers were only equipped with a pistol as a backup, if even that.

Short in length and fairly light in weight, the M79 proved extremely useful in the confining jungles of Vietnam. The M79 grenade launcher may also be known as the "Bloop Tube", "Blooper," "Thumper," or "Thump-Gun." In its current form, the M79 is in limited use around the globe, some seeing police duty in the crowd-control role.

One of the few completely new infantry weapons to appear during the Vietnam War, the M79 had no counterpart in the enemy's arsenal. It resembles a sawed-off shotgun and fires a spherical 40mm grenade which has a "kill radius" of five meters. Grooves in its barrel imparted a spiral spin to the warhead, stabilizing its flight. The spiral also caused weights in the fuse mechanism to arm the fuse after about 30 meters of flight, after which the shell detonated on impact. The grenades were thus safe from accidental detonation from a bump or fall, or if struck by a bullet.

Components

The major components of the 40-mm grenade launcher are shown in Figure 1-2. The front and rear sights, the safety, the trigger and trigger guard detent assembly, and the barrel-locking latch and lever are shown in Figures 1-3 through 1-8.

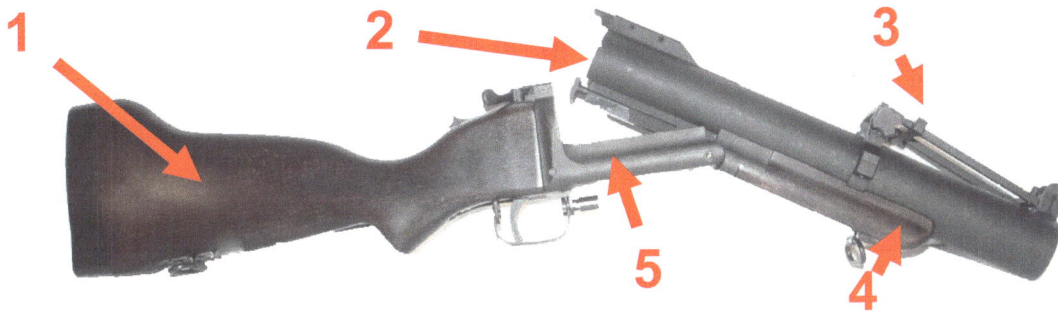

Figure 1-2 Relationship of components

1 – Stock Assembly
2 – Barrel Group
3 – Sight Assembly

4 – Fore-end Assembly
5 – Receiver Group

A. **Rear-Sight Assembly**. Figure 1-3 shows the adjustable rear-sight assembly, which consists of a rear-sight lock, a windage screw and scale, an elevation scale and lock screw, a sight carrier and retainer locknut, an elevating screw wheel and elevating screw, and a rear-sight frame with fixed leaf sight. To align the rear sight with the front sight, adjust the ladder on the rear sight. The M79 had a large flip-up sight situated halfway down the barrel, with a basic leaf foresight fixed at the end of the barrel. The rear sight was calibrated up to 375 meters (410 yds) in 25 meter (27.3 yds) intervals. In the hands of a good experienced grenadier, the M79 was highly accurate up to 200 meters.

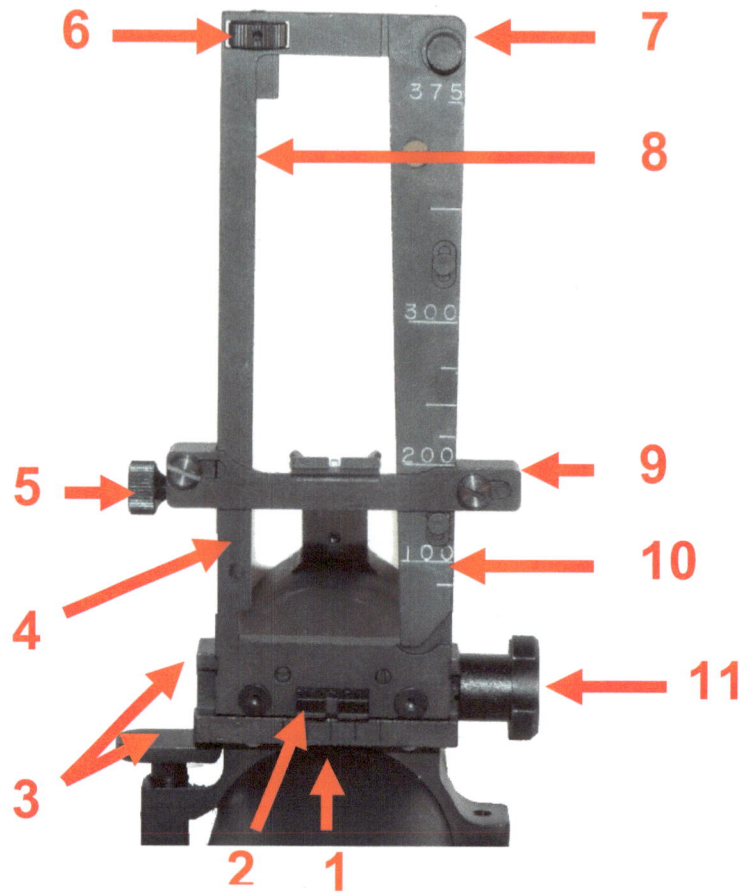

Figure 1-3 Rear sight

1 – Windage Scale
2 – Fixed Sight
3 – Sight Lock
4 – Sight Frame
5 – Sight Carrier Retainer Lock Nut
6 – Elevating Screw Wheel

7 – Elevation Scale Lock Screw
8 – Elevating Screw (hidden in photo)
9 – Sight Carrier
10 – Elevation Scale
11 – Windage Screw and Knob

1) **Rear-Sight Lock**. This lock is spring-loaded; you can lock the rear-sight frame assembly in either the UP or DOWN position. To unlock the sight frame, push down on the flat surface of the rear-sight lock. To relock the sight frame, release the pressure once the frame is in the desired position.

2) **Windage Screw and Windage Scale**. To adjust the rear sight for deflection, turn the knob on the right end of the windage screw. One click moves the impact of the grenade about 28 cm (11 inches) at a range of 200 meters. To adjust for right windage, turn the screw clockwise; for left windage, turn it counterclockwise. The windage scale has a zero line in its center and 10 equally spaced lines on each side of the zero line. You can move the rear sight assembly as much as 42 clicks right or left of center.

3) **Elevation Scale and Lock Screw**. The elevation scale is graduated from 75 to 375 meters in 25-meter increments and numbered at 100, 200, 300, and 375 meters. As you move the rear-sight carrier up the adjustable elevation scale, the rear sight cams to the left to compensate for the normal right-hand drift of the projectile. The lock screw holds the elevation scale in position.

4) **Sight Carrier Retainer Locknut**. Position and clamp the carrier to the sight frame in the desired position on the elevation scale. Turn the retainer locknut counterclockwise until you can push it inward. The inward pressure unlocks the sight carrier, which allows you to move it along the elevation scale. To lock the sight carrier in position, release the pressure on the retainer locknut and turn the nut clockwise until it stops.

5) **Elevating Screw and Screw Wheel**. Use the elevating screw and screw wheel to make fine adjustments in elevation. Turn the wheel clockwise to increase the elevation setting, counterclockwise to decrease it. Turning the screw moves the sight carrier along the elevation scale. One complete turn (one click) moves the impact of the round about 2 1/2 meters at a range of 200 meters.

6) **Rear-sight Frame with Fixed Sight**. When the rear sight frame is in the DOWN position, use the fixed sight to engage targets up to 100 meters away.

B. **Front Sight**. Figure A-4 shows the stationary front sight, which has a tapered blade and two blade guards.

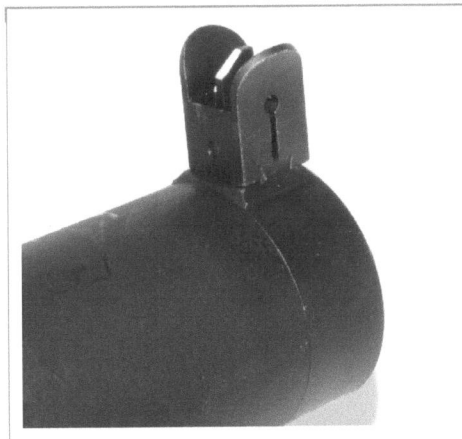

Figure 1-4 Front sight

C. **Safety**. To fire the launcher, ensure the safety is positioned forward (A, Figure 1-5) with the letter "F" visible near the rear of the safety. It will not fire if the letter "S" is visible. The safety automatically engages when you unlock the barrel-locking latch and open the breech (B, Figure 1-5).

**Figure 1-5A Safety engaged
SAFE Position**

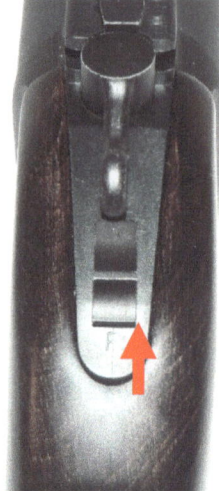

**Figure 1-4B Safety disengaged
FIRE Position**

D. **Trigger and Trigger-Guard Detent Assembly**. Figure A-6 shows the locations of the trigger and trigger guard. Depress the detent assembly to move the trigger guard right or left or to fire when wearing gloves or mittens.

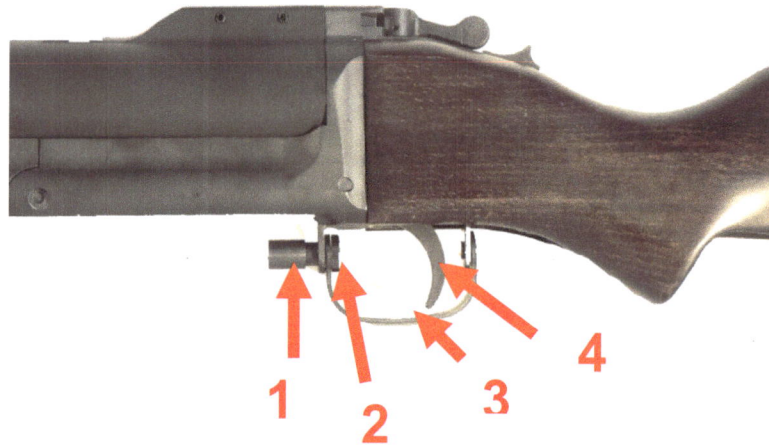

Figure 1-6 Position of trigger and trigger guard

1 – Detent Housing
2 – Detent Assembly

3 – Trigger Guard
4 – Trigger

E. **Barrel-locking Latch and Lever**. Figure 1-7 shows the barrel-locking latch on top of the receiver. This latch locks the barrel and the receiver together. To open (break) the breech end of the barrel, press the latch lever all the way to the right.

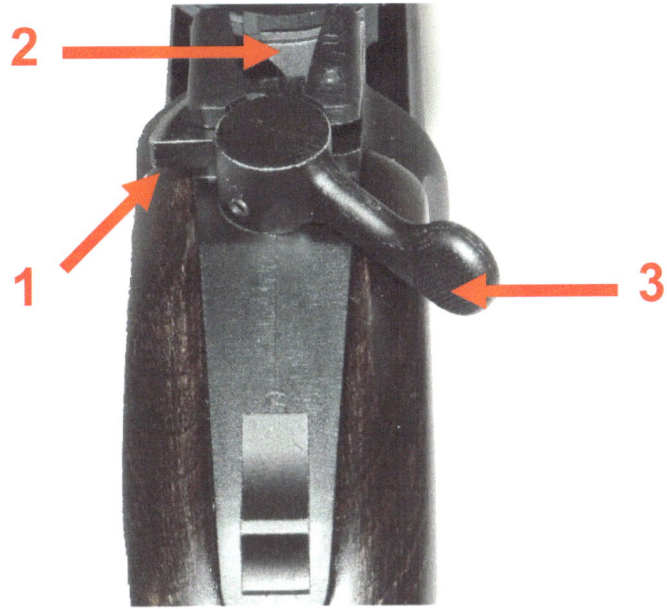

Figure 1-7 Operation of the barrel locking latch

1 – Barrel Locking Latch   3 – Barrel Locking Lever
2 – Barrel Locking Lug

Section 2

Maintenance

CLEARING PROCEDURE

Clearing the weapon is always the first step in performing maintenance or handling.

    A. Place the weapon on SAFE.

    B. Rotate the barrel-locking lever fully to the right.

    C. Open the barrel.

    D. Inspect the breech to ensure it is clear (no round is present).

    E. Return the barrel to the firing position.

CARE AND HANDLING

Proper maintenance of the M79 Grenade Launcher is vital and must be part of all gunnery training programs. Good maintenance contributes to weapon effectiveness, as well as to unit readiness. Maintaining the weapon includes clearing, disassembling, cleaning, lubricating, and inspecting it, and checking its assembly and functions.

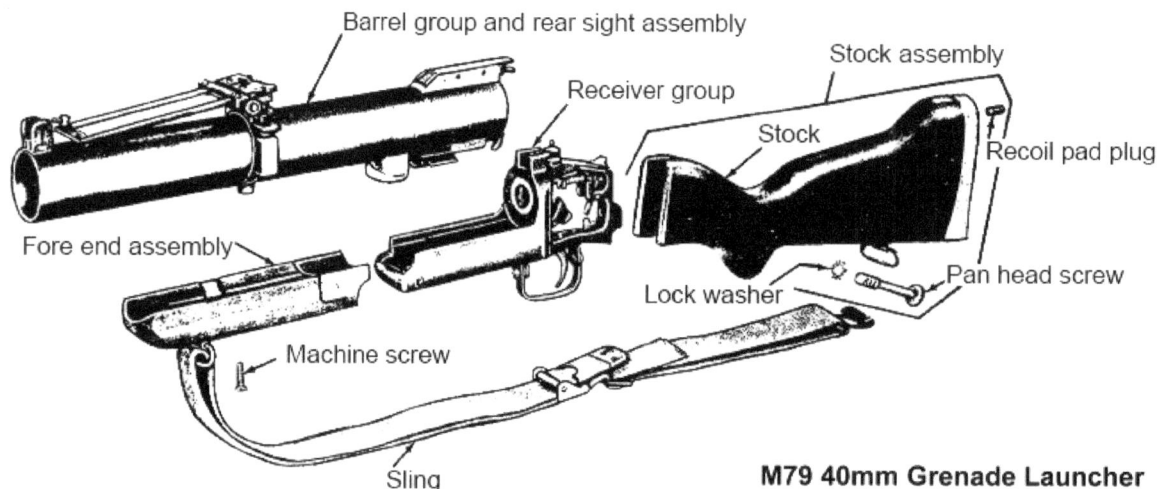

Figure 2-1 Exploded Diagram of the M79 GL

GENERAL DISASSEMBLY

The grenadier places each part he removes on a clean, flat surface (such as a table, shelter half, or disassembly mat) in the order they are removed. This assists in reassembly.

> **NOTE:** Ordnance personnel must disassemble the weapon beyond the level described in this paragraph.

A. Remove the sling from the stock.

B. Remove the retaining-band screw, which passes through the rear of the front sling swivel mount, and pull the fore-end assembly away from the barrel (Figure 2-2 and Figure 2-3).

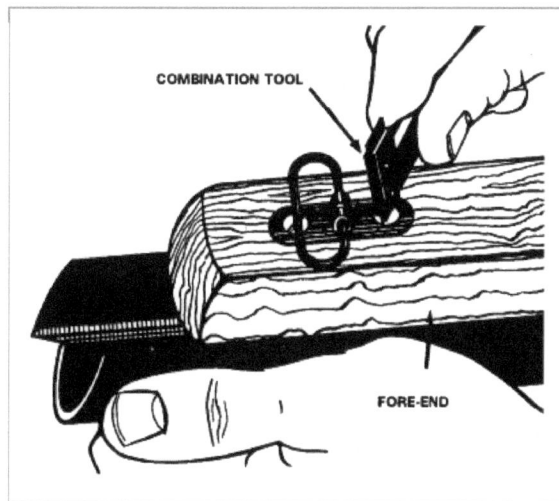

Figure 2-2 Removing or installing the retaining band screw

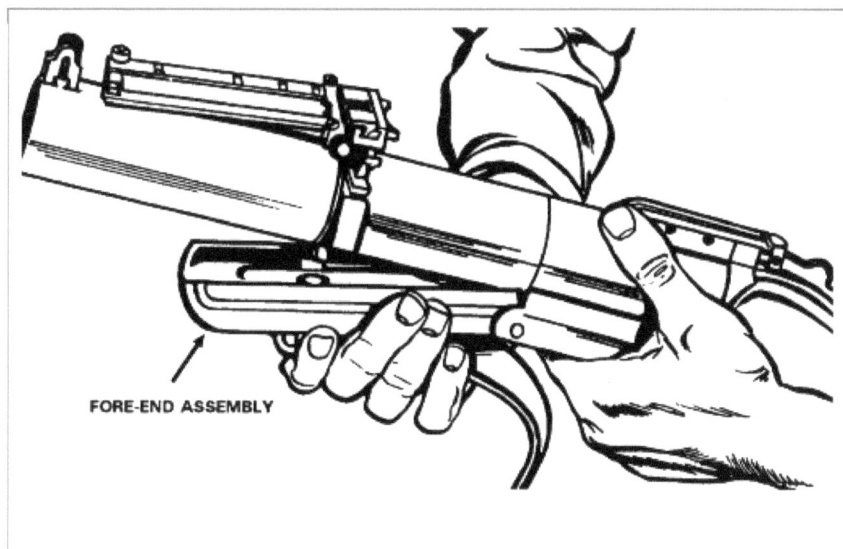

Figure 2-3 Removing or installing the fore-end assembly

C. Press the barrel-locking latch lever to the right and pivot the barrel down until it stops. Slide the barrel off the fulcrum pin and remove it from the receiver (Figure 2-4). Do not remove the rear sight from the barrel.

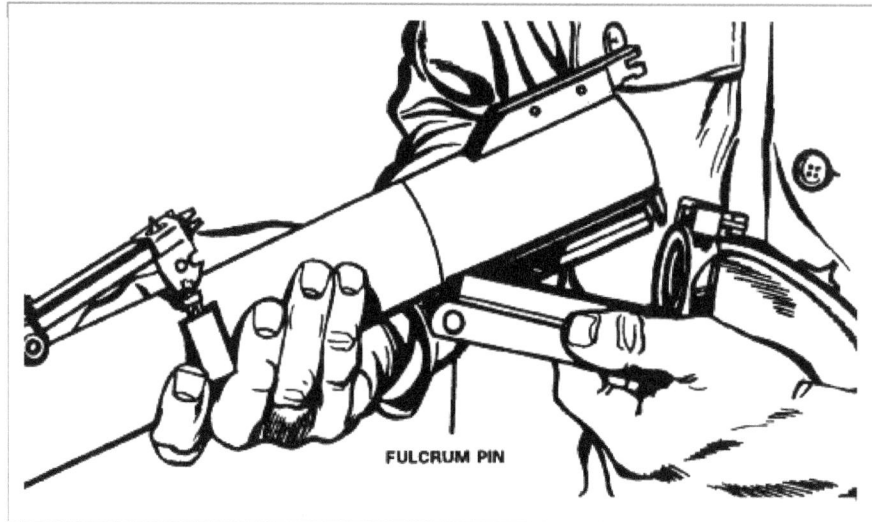

Figure 2-4 Removing or installing the barrel group

D. Remove the stock screw and washers and pull the stock rearward from the receiver (Figure 2-5).

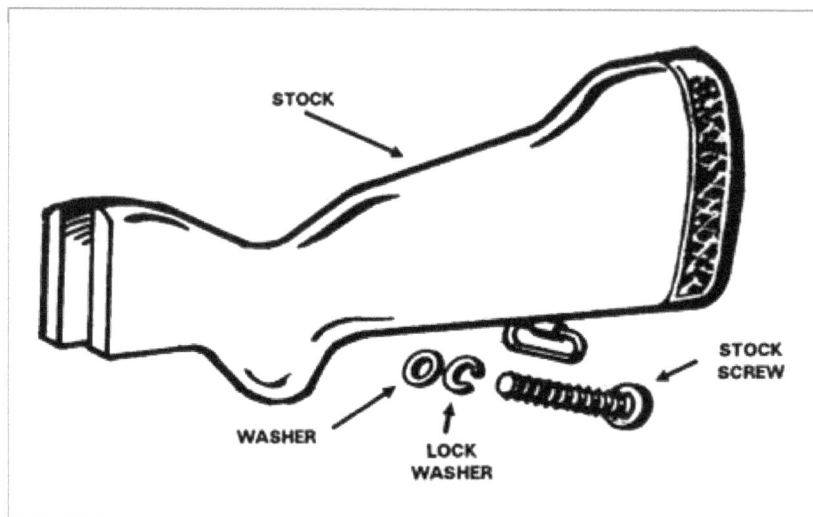

Figure 2-5 Removing the stock

Care and Handling

Certain steps must be taken before, during, and after firing to maintain the grenade launcher properly.

Before firing-
- Wipe the bore dry.
- Inspect the weapon as outlined in the operator's technical manual.
- Ensure the weapon is properly lubricated.

During firing-
- Periodically inspect the weapon to ensure that it is lubricated.
- When malfunctions or stoppages occur, follow the procedures outlined in Section 4.
- NOTE-- If fired into snow or mud, 40mm rounds may not hit hard enough to detonate. An undetonated round may explode when stepped on or driven over. During training in snow or mud, avoid this hazard by firing only TP rounds.
- Ensure sufficient overhead clearance exists for indirect fire. Remember that some rounds arm themselves 14 to 28 meters from the muzzle of the launcher.

Cleaning and Lubrication
1. **Bore.** Attach a clean, dry rag to the thong and thoroughly moisten the rag with Cleaner, Lubricant, and Protectant (CLP). Pull the rag through the bore several times. Attach the bore brush to the thong, pull it through the bore several times, and follow this with more rags moistened with CLP. Pull dry rags through the bore, and inspect each rag as it is removed. The bore is clean when a dry rag comes out clean. Finally, pull a rag lightly moistened with CLP through the bore to leave a light coat of lubricant inside the barrel. The best option to clean the bore is a BH-34040 40mm Boresnake pull-through cleaner, which has a built-on brass brush and swab for one pass cleaning (Figure 2-6).

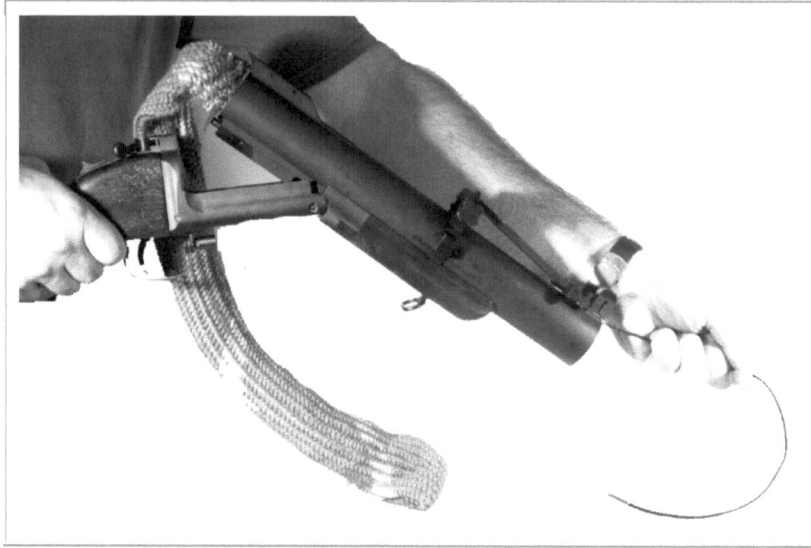

Figure 2-6 Cleaning the barrel with a bore snake

2. **Breech Insert**. Clean the face of the breech insert with a patch and CLP. Remove this CLP with dry rags; then lubricate the breech with a new light coat of CLP.

3. **Other Parts**. Use a brush and dry rags to clean all the other parts and surfaces. After cleaning, apply a light coat of CLP to the outside of the launcher.

4. **Safety Mechanism**. Clean the safety mechanism properly with CLP; then lubricate it with CLP.

5. **Special Lubrication Requirements**. Keep the weapon clean and lubed with a CLP. Lubricate the grenade launcher only with CLP and IAW the following environmental guidelines:

   A. **Extreme Heat**. Lubricate with CLP, grade 2.

   B. **Damp or Salty Air**. Clean the weapon and apply CLP, grade 2, frequently. Rainy, humid, and salty air contaminate the lube and cause corrosion. Inspect grenade launcher daily. Dry, clean, and lubricate as necessary.

   C. **Sandy or Dusty Air**. Clean the weapon and apply CLP, grade 2, frequently. Remove excess CLP with a rag after each application. Clean often. Oil frequently because heat dissolves the oil rapidly. Wipe oil from exposed surfaces. Cover weapon as much as possible. Keep sand out of parts.

D. **Temperatures below Freezing**. When the weapon is brought in from a cold area to a warm area, keep it wrapped in a parka or blanket, and allow it to reach room temperature gradually. If condensation forms on the weapon, dry and lubricate it at room temperature with CLP, grade 2, before returning it to cold weather. Otherwise, ice will form inside the mechanism.

E. **After immersion in water,** disassemble, clean, oil, and reassemble as soon as possible. Make sure launcher is dry.

Inspecting the M79 Grenade Launcher

1. Inspection begins with the weapon already disassembled into its major groups or assemblies. Parts with shiny surfaces are serviceable.

   A. **All Parts**. Check for wear, corrosion, moisture, foreign matter and damage, including burrs, scratches, dents, and nicks.

   B. **Leaf Sight Assembly**. Check for bent or damaged parts, rust or corrosion, and illegibility of markings.

   C. **Barrel**. Check for cracks or dents.

   D. **Cartridge and Retainers**. Check for breakage, bends, chips, or missing parts.

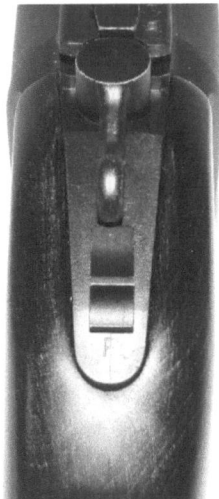

Check safe and fire positions   Check locking lever and locking latch
Figure 2-7 Points to inspect

GENERAL ASSEMBLY

The grenadier should assemble the grenade launcher in the reverse order in which he disassembled it.

A. Place the lock washer on the stock screw and install the stock on the receiver.

B. Place the barrel on the fulcrum pin. Hold the cocking lever up, lower the barrel, and ensure that the cocking arm slides under the cocking lever. Close the barrel.

C. Place the fore-end assembly on the barrel and secure it by replacing the retaining-band screw.

D. Replace the sling.

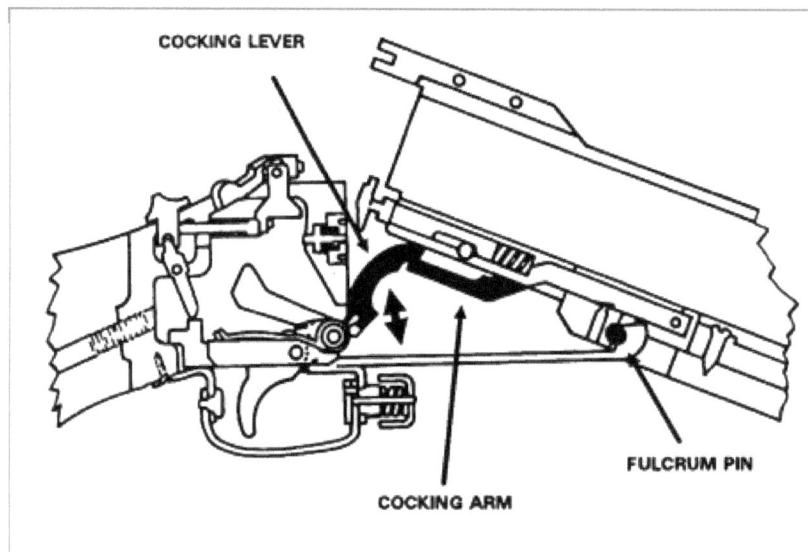

Figure 2-8 Assembling the barrel and receiver groups

Performing a Function Check on the M79 Grenade Launcher

A. Always perform the function check with out ammunition nearby and pointed in a safe direction.

B. Press the safety to the rear SAFE position (exposing "S").

C. Press the trigger (the hammer should not fall).

D. Press the safety to the forward FIRE position (exposing "F").

E. Press the trigger (the hammer should fall).

F. Open the launcher to recock, ensure the safety is on SAFE and close the breech.

Section 3

Operation and Function

CLEARING PROCEDURE

Clearing the weapon is always the first step in performing maintenance or handling.

    A. Place the weapon on SAFE.

    B. Rotate the barrel locking lever fully to the right.

    C. Open the barrel.

    D. Inspect the breech to ensure it is clear (no round is present).

    E. Return the barrel to the firing position.

Operations include loading, unloading, and firing the weapon, which uses a high-low propulsion system to fire a round. The firing pin strikes the primer, and its flash ignites the propellant in the brass powder-charge cup inside the high-pressure chamber. The burning propellant produces 35,000 psi chamber pressure, which ruptures the brass powder-charge cup at the vent holes. This allows the gases to escape to the low-pressure chamber in the cartridge case, where the pressure drops to 3,000 psi and propels the grenade from the muzzle at a velocity of 250 fps. The grenade's 37,000-rpm right-hand spin stabilizes the grenade during flight and applies enough rotational force to arm the fuze. The grenadier loads and unloads the weapon with the barrel open and fires it from a closed receiver. **The launcher must be cocked before it can be placed on SAFE**.

    A. **Loading**. To load the weapon (Figure 3-1)—

    1) Move the barrel-locking latch as far to the right as possible; pull down on the front of the barrel group.

    2) Insert a round into the chamber, ensuring the extractor contacts the cartridge case rim.

    3) Close the weapon by rotating the barrel group up on the pivot point.

    4) Place the weapon on SAFE.

Figure 3-1 Loading the grenade launcher

WARNING - Keep the muzzle pointed downrange and clear of all soldiers. Use the correct ammunition; <u>never use high-velocity 40mm ammunition</u>.

B. **Unloading**. To unload the weapon (Figure 3-2)—

1) Place the weapon on SAFE by moving the barrel-locking latch as far right as possible.

2) If the cartridge case is partially extracted, remove the cartridge case. If the cartridge case is not partially extracted, engage the extractor tang and pull it rearward.

3) Grasp the cartridge case and remove it.

Figure 3-2 Unloading the grenade launcher

WARNING
If you are unloading a weapon that has not been fired, avoid detonation either by catching the ejected round or by holding the weapon close to the ground to reduce the distance the round can fall.

CYCLE OF FUNCTIONING

Understanding how the weapon functions helps grenadiers recognize and correct stoppages. The loading and firing of a round and the resulting effect on the parts of the weapon are referred to as the cycle of functioning. Many of the actions in this cycle occur at the same time and are separated here only to explain them more clearly.

A. **Unlocking**. Before you can unlock the barrel from the receiver and move the safety to the SAFE position, you must press the barrel-locking latch lever all the way to the right. The spring-loaded latch lock holds the barrel locking latch open (Figure 3-1).

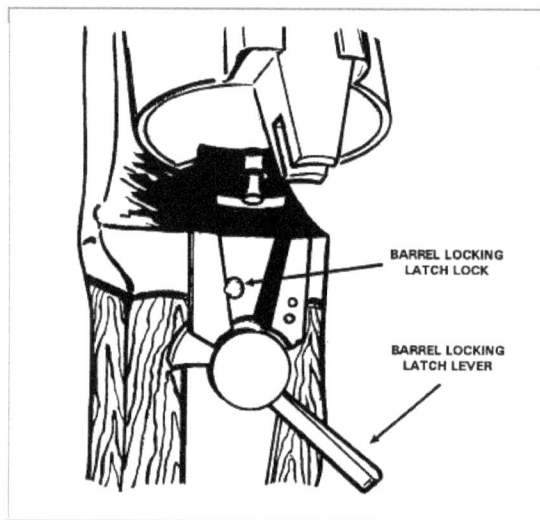

Figure 3-3 Barrel release latch lock and barrel locking latch lever

B. **Cocking**. Opening the barrel cocks the weapon by causing the cocking arm to lift the cocking lever. The cocking lever rotates around the hammer pin until it contacts a stud on the hammer. Then the lever rotates upward with the hammer until the sear engages the sear notch, cocking the weapon.

C. **Extracting**. Extraction occurs while you are cocking the weapon (Figure 3-4). As you open the barrel, the spring-loaded extractor withdraws the spent cartridge case about 1/2 inch from the breech end of the barrel.

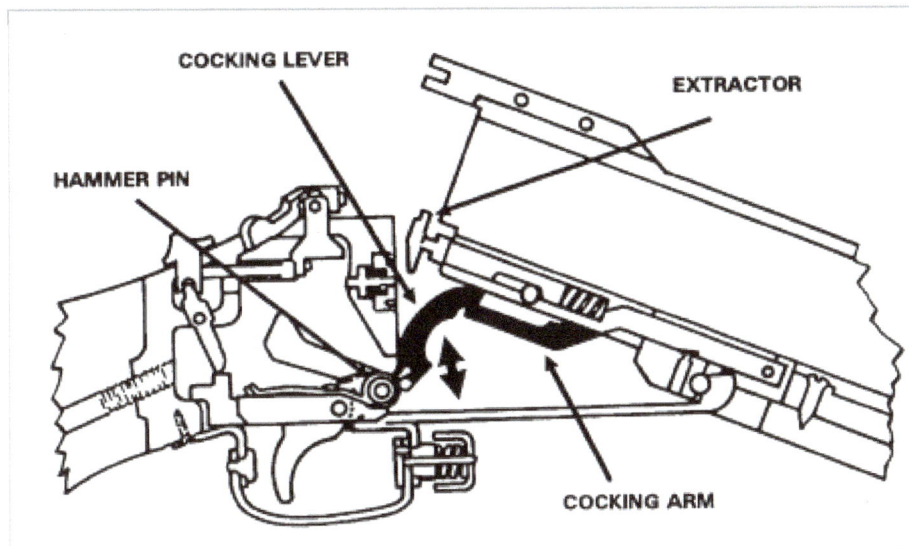

Figure 3-4 Cocking the weapon and extracting a round or cartridge case

D. **Ejecting**. The M79 grenade launcher does not eject rounds automatically; you must remove the expended cartridge case or live round from the barrel (Figure 3-5).

E. **Loading**. With the barrel in the open position, insert a cartridge into the breech end of the barrel (Figure 3-5).

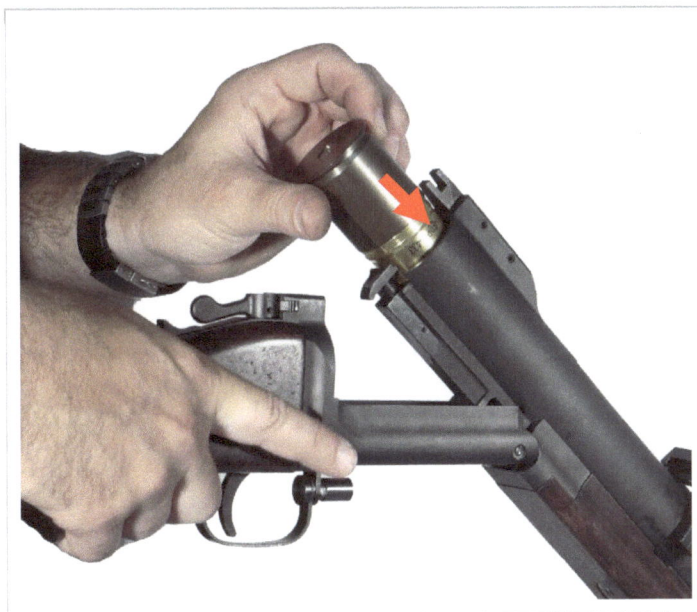

Figure 3-5 Loading the weapon or ejecting a round or cartridge case

F. **Chambering**. Closing the barrel forces the extractor into the extractor housing, which causes the cartridge to seat in the chamber.

G. **Locking**. Closing the barrel also depresses the latch lock, which rotates until it locks the barrel to the receiver (when it engages the barrel-locking lug). Before firing the weapon, you must push the safety forward to expose the letter "F."

H. **Firing**. As you pull the trigger rearward, it rotates on the trigger pin. The rear of the trigger lifts the rear of the sear, causing the nose of the sear to disengage from the sear notch in the hammer. This releases the spring-driven hammer, which strikes the firing pin and drives it forward to strike the primer of the cartridge. When you release the trigger, the hammer settles back slightly, allowing the firing pin spring to withdraw the pin from the face of the retainer (Figure 3-6).

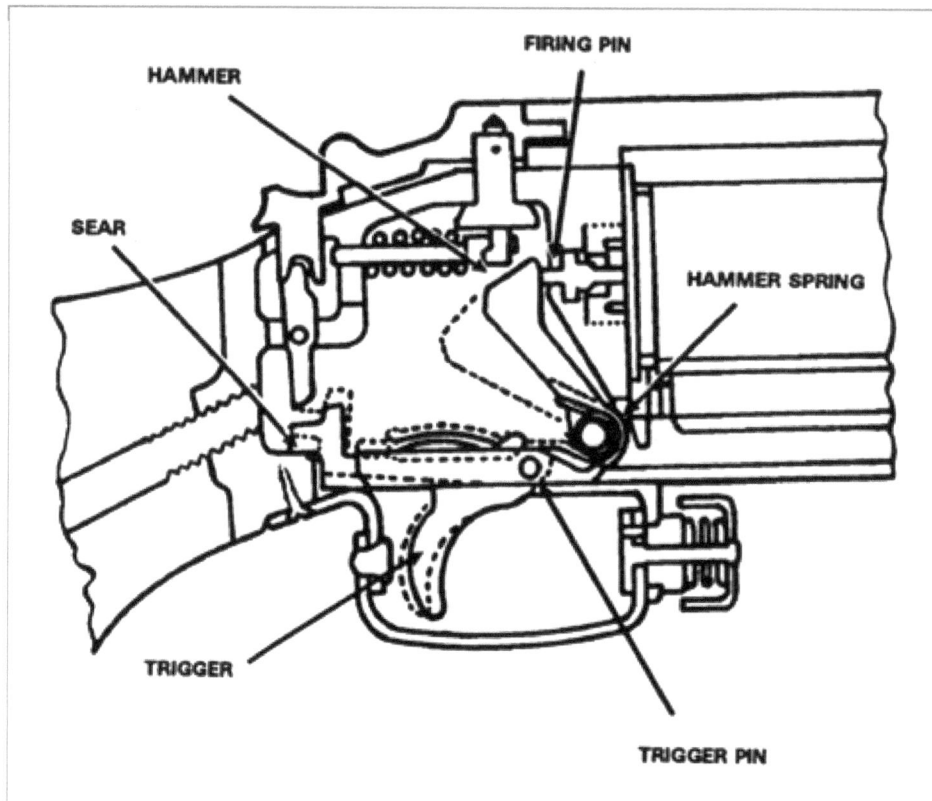

Figure 3-6 Firing the weapon

Marksmanship

Marksmanship training teaches the grenadier to fire the grenade launcher and prepares him to employ it in combat. Except for the subjects discussed in the remainder of this section, marksmanship training, range construction, and range firing are the same for the M79 grenade launcher as they are for the M203 Grenade Launcher. **After approximately 15 meters of flight, the grenade is armed**.

A. **Sight Alignment, Sight Picture, and Sight Manipulation**. Sight alignment is the relationship between the front-sight blade and the rear-sight notch. Figure 3-7 shows the correct sight alignment. If you drew an imaginary horizontal line across the top of the rear-sight notch, the top of the front-sight blade would touch the line. If you drew an imaginary vertical line through the center of the notch, the line would cut the front-sight blade in half. Sight picture includes sight alignment and the placement of the aiming point (Figure 3-8). Sight manipulation means placing the rear-sight carrier at the elevation-scale setting that corresponds to the range to the target.

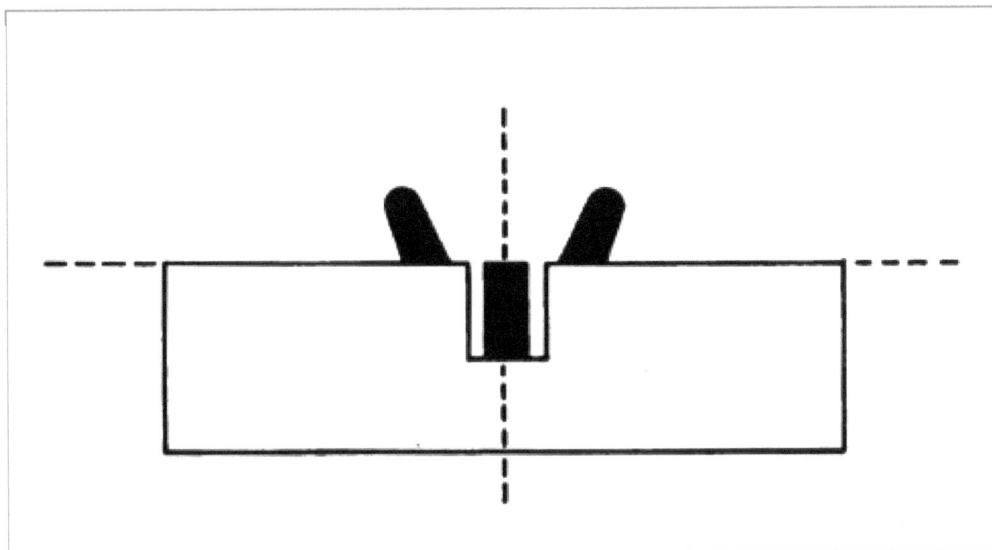

Figure 3-7 Correct sight alignment

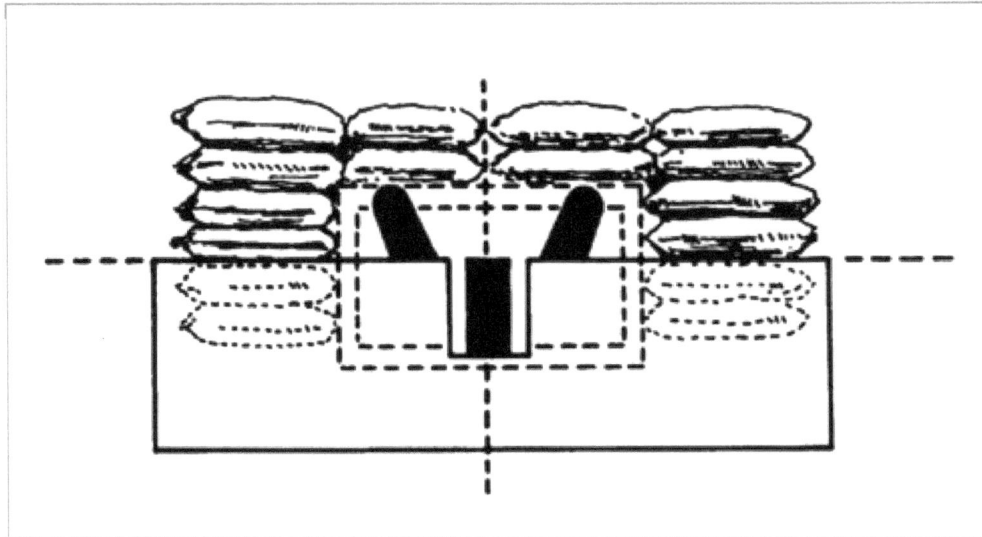

Figure 3-8 Correct sight picture

B. **Positions**. You are most likely to use are the prone, kneeling, and standing positions. When you have an option, always use the more stable supported positions. Using the M79 in firing positions differs from using the M203 in the following ways:

1) Assume firing positions the same as you would with your service rifle, but hold your right thumb against the right side of the grenade launcher's stock. If you place this thumb over the small of the stock, the safety can injure your thumb, and you will not achieve a spot weld with the grenade launcher.

2) Several actions are common to all the firing positions for the M79 grenade launcher:

   a. Rest the launcher across the heel of your left hand, in the V formed by your left thumb and forefinger.
   b. Relax the fingers of your left hand, and place your hand so that the upper sling swivel cannot pinch it, or blood, swearing and scarring will occur.
   c. Keep your left wrist straight, with your left thumb resting against the fore-end assembly -- not on the rear sight base. Placing your thumb near the rear sight base could cause injury during firing.
   d. Place your left elbow under the launcher.
   e. Position your right elbow far enough to the right to level your shoulders and far enough forward to form a good pocket for the butt of the launcher.
   f. Rest the thumb of your right hand along the side of the stock.

> **WARNING**
> **Do not place your thumb over the small of the stock. The safety could injure your thumb when the launcher recoils.**

  g. Place your trigger finger on the trigger so that your finger and the side of the stock do not touch.
  h. Regardless of the firing position you have chosen, try to relax.

3) At ranges less than 150 meters, you can fire normally from your shoulder in any position. However, to maintain sight alignment at greater ranges, lower the position of the stock on your shoulder or drop the butt from your shoulder. At near-maximum ranges, you must position the stock between your waist and your armpit and hold the stock firmly against your body with your upper arm. In the prone position, once the stock is no longer against your shoulder, rest the butt of the launcher on the ground. Be careful to keep your head level when your cheek breaks contact with the stock. Figure 3-9 shows the changes that occur as the range to the target increases.

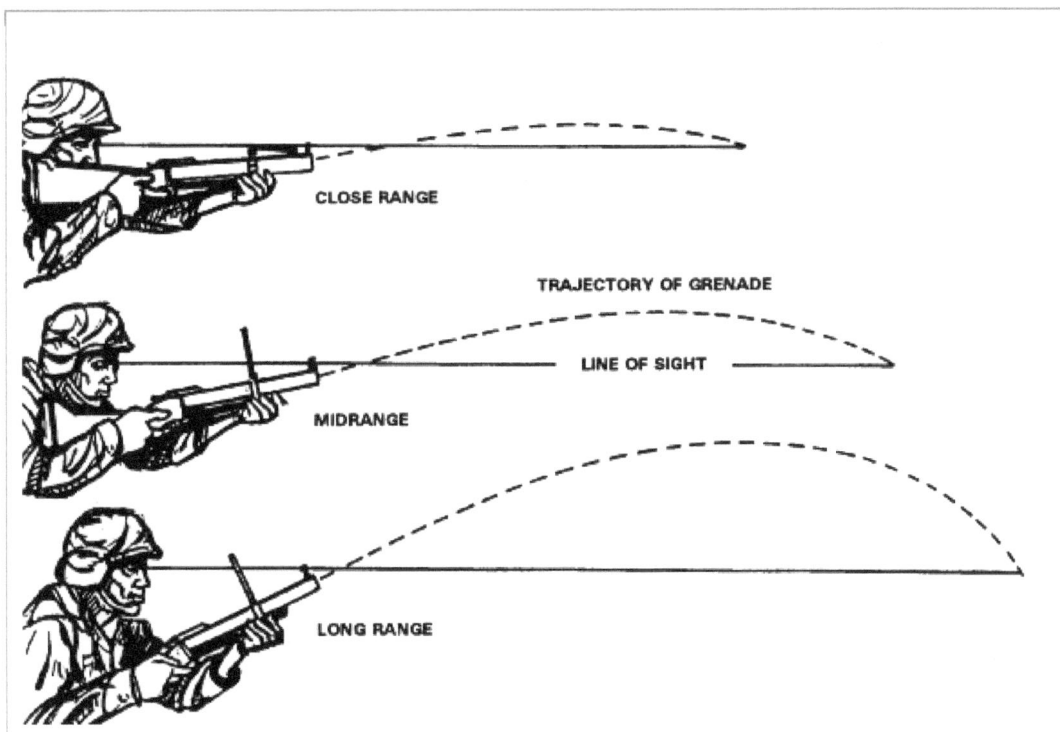

Figure 3-9 Effect of increasing range

4) When pinpoint accuracy is not required, use the pointing technique to deliver a high rate of HE fire (Figure 3-10). The pointing technique uses a modified underarm firing position without using the sights. Keep both eyes open, concentrate on the target, and keep the muzzle of the launcher in position so you can easily adjust your fire. This technique is

most useful in an assault because it allows you to reload rapidly with your left hand. However, you can use it in any standard firing position.

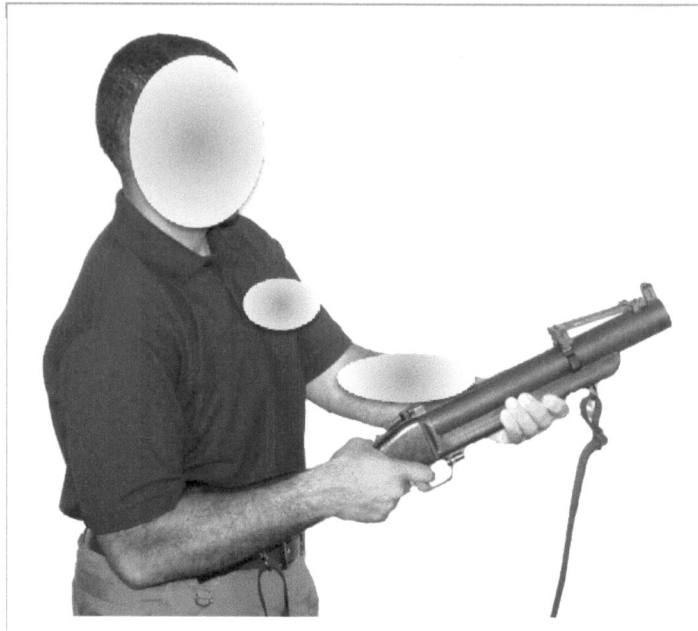

Figure 3-10 Pointing technique

I. **Zeroing Procedure**. You have achieved a correct zero for a given range when your elevation and windage settings enable you to hit the point of aim. To zero the M79 Grenade Launcher, engage a target at 200 meters. This range allows you the most flexibility to adjust elevation.

1) Place the rear sight's center index line on the windage scale's center mark.

2) Unlock the elevation scale by turning its lock screw counterclockwise. Position the top of the scale flush with the top of the sight frame and relock the scale. To unlock the rear-sight carrier, turn and push the locknut that retains it. Slide the carrier along the elevation scale until the 200-meter index on the scale aligns with the top edge of the sight carrier. Relock the rear-sight carrier.

3) Assume a prone supported position and align the target with the front and rear sights, using correct sighting and aiming procedure.

4) Fire a round, sense the impact of the grenade, and adjust the sight.

   a. **Elevation**. Turn the elevation screw wheel clockwise to increase the range, counterclockwise to decrease. At a range of 200 meters, one click on the wheel moves the impact of the grenade 2 1/2 meters.

b. **Windage**. Turn the windage knob clockwise to move the impact of the grenade to the right, or counterclockwise to move left. At a range of 200 meters, one click on the knob moves the impact of the grenade about 11 inches.

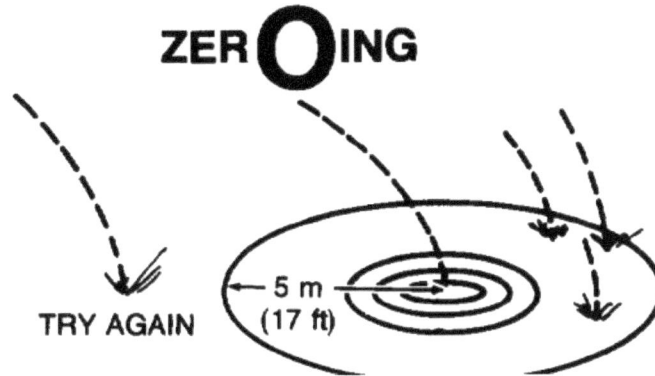

ZER⬤ING

TRY AGAIN   ← 5 m
(17 ft)

5) Fire two more rounds, and adjust after each. If the last round lands within 5 meters of the target, the weapon is correctly zeroed.

6) After confirming the zero, move the elevation scale so that the 200-meter index line is flush with the top of the sight carrier.

INDIRECT FIRE ROLE

Although the M79 grenade launcher is designed for direct fire, it can be used to place HE fragmentation fire on area targets that cannot be observed.

A. **Employment**. The accuracy of the weapon is limited in the indirect fire role. Adjust the range, in 25-meter increments, to a maximum range of about 400 meters.

B. **Sighting System**. The standard sight assembly is graduated up to 375 meters, which corresponds to a 32-degree elevation. However, you can raise the rear sight carrier to increase elevation to up to 40 degrees. The rear sight cannot be used at greater elevations. The most accurate way to fire the M79 grenade launcher in the indirect fire mode is to attach an M15 rifle grenade sight to the weapon's stock (Figure 3-11). This sight consists of a mounting scale plate and sight bar assembly.

Figure 3-11 Using the M5 rifle grenade sight

1) Installing the M15 Sight. To prevent the wood in the launcher's stock from cracking when the sight is installed, hold the sight against the stock and mark the positions for the screws. Drill two pilot holes. Use two short wood screws and attach the mounting plate to the side of the stock. Ensure they do not protrude through the stock since this will make disassembling the weapon difficult.

2) **Adjusting the M15 Sight**. Once you attach the M15 sight to the M79 Grenade Launcher, you will no longer need to use the mounting plate's degree scale. Place a short piece of masking tape on the stock above the mounting plate. Adjust your fires until the rounds impact at the desired range. After you determine the sight setting, draw a line on the tape along the top of the sight bar. Label each line for the appropriate range. Fire several rounds to determine the M15 sight-elevation graduation required to fire the desired range. Mark this graduation on the stock for quick reference.

3) **Using the M15 Sight**. Align the launcher for deflection. Assume a correct firing position, sight over or along the barrel, and move the launcher to align the barrel toward the target. Ensure the weapon is not canted. Raise or lower the muzzle to center the leveling bubble and determine the angle of elevation. If you have enough light, using the M15 sight is the quickest, easiest way to determine the proper angle of elevation.

C. **Adjustments for Elevation and Deflection**. To bring indirect fire rounds nearer the target, move the barrel slightly for elevation or deflection.

1) **Elevation**. Estimate the range to the target and move the barrel either up or down. Table 3-1 provides guidelines to help you set the proper elevation.

Range	Elevation	Distance from Front Sling Swivel to Ground
200 meters	69 degrees	21 1/4 inches
300 meters	8 degrees	19 3/8 inches
400 meters	41 degrees	12 1/4 inches

Table 3-1 Range estimation and elevation

2) **Deflection**. Sight over or along the barrel at an aiming point. To increase the accuracy of indirect fire, place a string or straight stick on the ground in line with an aiming point or stake.

D. **Ammunition**. Because live ammunition must be conserved during both training and combat, TP rounds are used for training and zeroing. A TP round emits a puff of orange or yellow smoke on impact, which will help you adjust fire. TP rounds produce little fragmentation, which reduces the possibility of a training injury.

E. **Wind and Other Weather Effects**. Firing any 40mm grenade launcher round in the indirect-fire role doubles the time required for the round to reach the target. This allows wind, snow, and rain twice the time to push the projectile off its normal trajectory. Before firing, you must evaluate and compensate for the wind, whether it is a crosswind or is blowing on the same axis as the grenade. This evaluation (referred to as "Kentucky windage") increases the chance of a first-round hit and reduces the chance that a round will impact closer to you than desired. Be careful when a wind of 5 mph or more is blowing from the direction of the target. Consider this particular wind condition when firing at all ranges, but remember that it presents the greatest danger at the minimum indirect fire range of 200 meters.

F. **Fire Control**. You may fire indirectly only when you receive a specific command to do so.

1) Fire commands for indirect fire differ from those for direct fire only in that INDIRECT FIRE is given as the method of employment right after the target and range are designated.
   - "GRENADIER"
   - "FRONT"
   - "INDIRECT FIRE, 3 ROUNDS"
   - "TROOPS IN OPEN"
   - "AT MY COMMAND"

2) If the indirect fire target is not visible from where you are, the squad leader may employ an observer.

3) Grenade launcher fire-for-effect should always consist of three to five rounds, depending on the nature of the target.

G. **Firing Positions**. You may fire the M79 Grenade Launcher indirectly from the kneeling, sitting, or squatting position.

1) **Kneeling**. The kneeling position for indirect fire is about the same as for direct fire (Figure 3-12).
   a. Face the target and kneel on your right knee (if you are firing right-handed), keeping your left foot pointed in the direction of the target.
   b. Sit on your right heel and place the butt of the stock on the ground against or alongside your right knee.
   c. With your left hand, grasp the launcher near the upper sling swivel. With your right, grasp the small of the stock. Your right thumb should be parallel to your trigger finger and against the right side of the stock. The weight of your body should rest on your right heel.

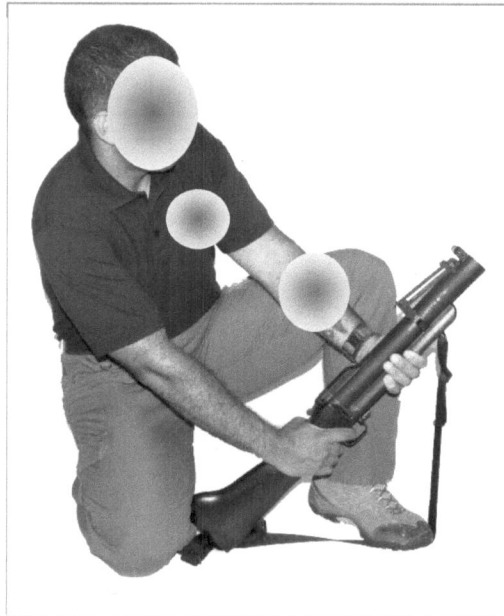

Figure 3-12 Kneeling position using the marked-sling method

2) **Sitting**. The sitting position for indirect fire is about the same as for direct fire. Use this position with aiming stakes or with the M15 sight (Figure 3-13).

a. Keep your right leg flat on the ground and pointed at the target, crossing your left leg over your knee so your left knee supports your left elbow.
b. Place the butt of the stock alongside your right hip.
c. Hold the weapon as described for the indirect-fire kneeling position.

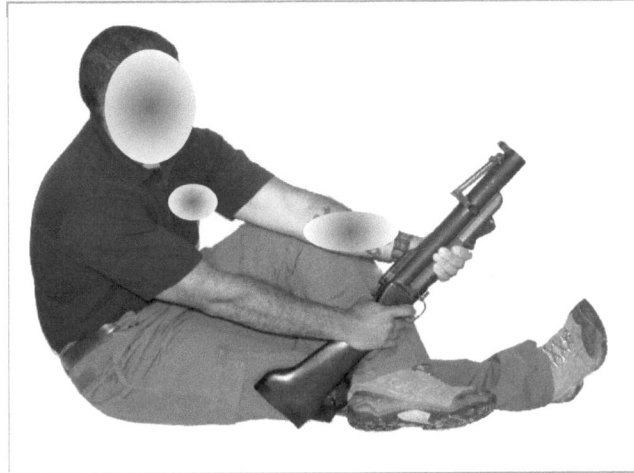

Figure 3-13 Sitting position for indirect fire

3) **Squatting**. If you must remain in an indirect fire position for any length of time, squatting is the least comfortable. It is identical to the direct fire modified squatting position except for one difference: place the weapon between your knees, with the butt of the stock on the ground (Figure 3-14). Hold the launcher as described for the kneeling position. Use aiming stakes or the M15 sight with this position.

Figure 3-14 Squatting position for indirect fire

H. **Methods of Fire**. Three methods may be used to fire the M79 indirectly.

1) **Marked-Sling Method**. This is the most field-expedient method. Loosen the sling, assume a kneeling position, and place your forward foot in the sling (Figure A-24). Before firing, ensure that the sling is taut and vertical between the front sling swivel and your boot. If not, the rounds will impact at a greater range than you desire. To ensure the sling is vertical, tie one end of a piece of string to the front sling swivel and the other end to a weight such as a cartridge case. Align the edge of the sling with the string. Fire several rounds to determine the desired range. Use tape, paint, ink, or a similar material to mark the sling where your foot is holding it to the ground. Mark the position of the sling keeper and buckle so that if either is moved, you can return it to its original position to ensure constant range accuracy. Remember that the sling may stretch or shrink if it gets wet, which will increase or decrease the range to impact.

2) **Aiming Stakes Method**. If you use aiming stakes, you can deliver planned indirect fire (Figure 3-15). Place the aiming stakes and verify their alignment in daylight. Record planned fires on a range card or sector sketch. Then place the fore-end assembly of the weapon on top of an elevation support, scooping a slight depression out of the ground for the toe of the weapon's stock. Adjust the weapon for the range desired; then drive a stake into the ground behind the toe of the stock to absorb recoil and prevent the weapon from digging into the ground. To control the barrel's lateral movement, place two deflection stakes behind the front elevation support. Place another elevation support beneath the stock of the weapon and two more deflection stakes behind the support to control the stock's lateral movement. Place the deflection stakes closer together than the front stakes.

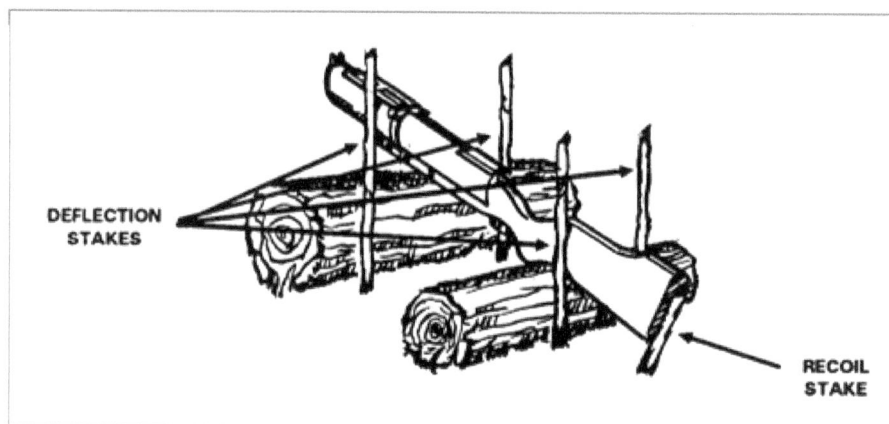

Figure 3-15 Planned fires using aiming stakes

I. Safety Precautions. The grenadier should observe the following safety precautions in addition to those stated in established range regulations and in local range regulations:

1) Keep your head behind and below the muzzle of the launcher when firing.
2) Ensure sufficient overhead clearance exists for indirect fire. Remember that some rounds arm themselves 14 to 28 meters from the muzzle of the launcher.
3) Fire no rounds at less than 200 meters in training with non training rounds.

Characteristics of fire

The characteristics of fire discussed in this section are defined as follows:

1. **Trajectory-** This is the curve described in space by the fired round as it travels to its target. The trajectory rises as the sights are elevated.

2. **Line of Sight-** This is an imaginary line from the gun to the target, as seen through properly adjusted sights.

3. **Ordinate-** This is the vertical distance at any point between the trajectory and the line of sight.

4. **Maximum Ordinate-** This is the greatest vertical distance between the trajectory and the line of sight; it occurs at the highest point of the trajectory.

5. **Danger Space-** This is the area where the round impact or the shrapnel from the round impact injures personnel or destroys the target.

6. **Dead Space-** This is the area(s) where personnel or targets are safe from direct-fire weapons. Ditches, depressions, and ravines are examples of dead spaces.

Classes of fire

Fire distribution is classified three ways:

1. **With Respect to the Ground-** For the M79 Grenade Launcher, this class of fire refers only to plunging fire. Plunging fire occurs when firing at long ranges, from high ground to low ground, into abruptly rising ground, or across uneven terrain, resulting in a loss of grazing fire at any point along the trajectory. For example, 40mm grenades fired from the top of a hill follow an arcing trajectory and land in the valley. Figure 3-16 shows an example of plunging fire.

2. **With Respect to the Target.** This includes four ways to distribute fire (Figure 3-17):
    A. **Frontal-** Frontal fire is directed against a target's front, with the target facing or moving toward the firing position.
    B. **Flanking-** Flanking fire is directed against the target's flank.
    C. **Oblique-** Oblique fire is directed against a target moving or facing at an angle rather than directly toward or perpendicular to the gun.
    D. **Enfilade-** Enfilade fire is directed along the length of a target and may be frontal or flanking, depending on which way the target is facing.

Figure 3-16 Plunging fire

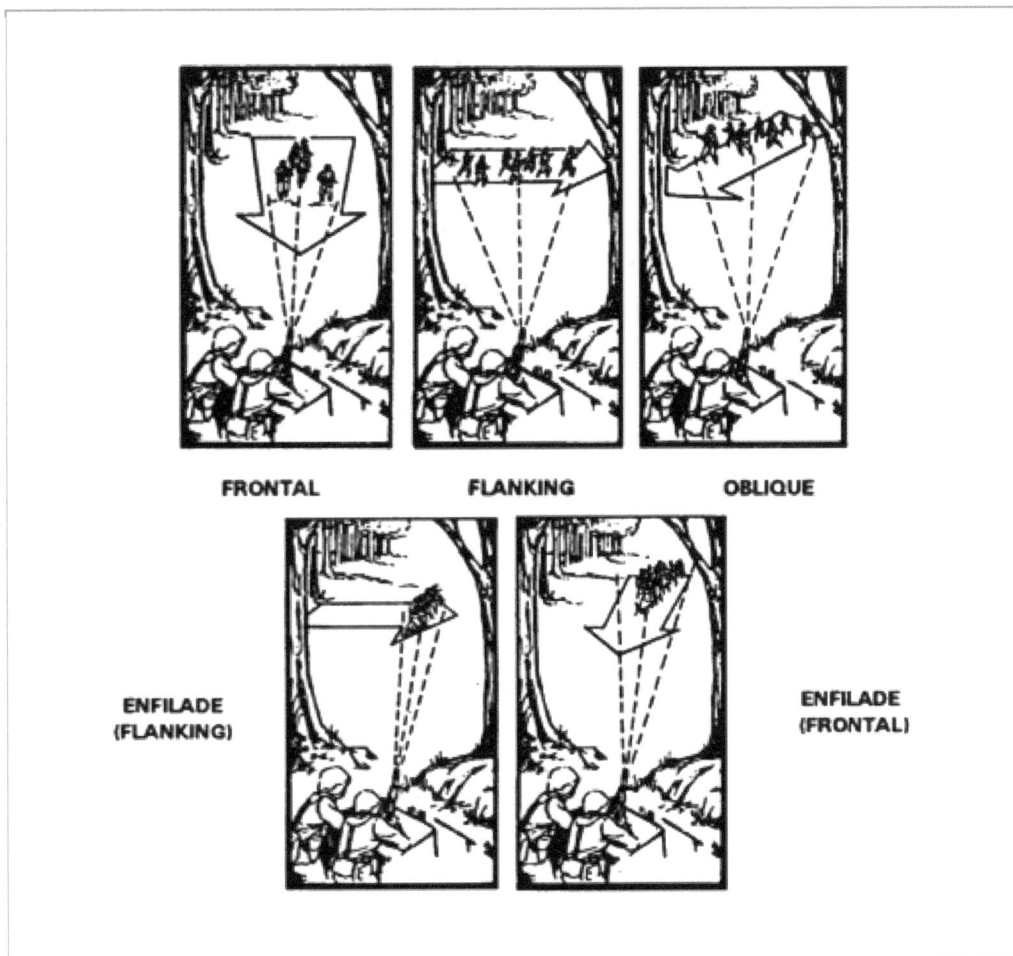

FRONTAL   FLANKING   OBLIQUE

ENFILADE (FLANKING)   ENFILADE (FRONTAL)

Figure 3-17 Classes of fire with respect to the target

3. **With Respect to the Weapon**. This also includes four ways to distribute fire (Figure 3-19):

     A. **Rapid Fire Point**- Distribute fire against a target with one aim point.

B. **Rapid Fire Right or Left-** Distribute fire right to left or left to right without changing range. Use this against frontal or flanking targets.

C. **Rapid Fire Searching-** Distribute fire against a deep target changing elevation but not direction. Use this fire against enfilade targets.

D. **Rapid Fire Right or Left and Searching-** Distribute fire against a target with depth and width changing elevation and direction. Use this fire against an oblique target.

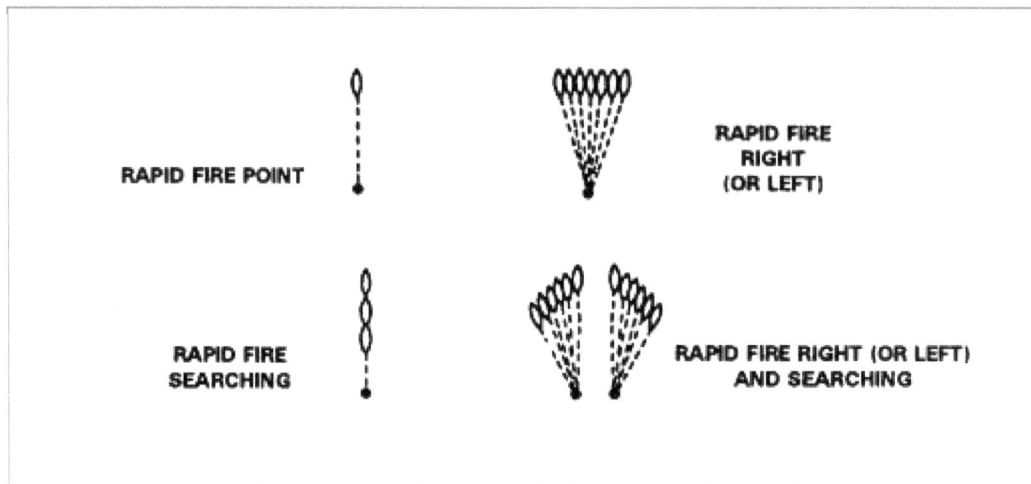

Figure 3-19 Classes of fire with respect to the weapon

Range estimation

The operator must be able to estimate range. This estimation enables him to hit targets with the first round and to adjust and shift fire if necessary. He often estimates range visually, using one of three methods:

1. **100-Meter Unit-of-Measurement Method-** Visualize 100 meters on the ground (this takes practice). Then estimate how many 100-meter units lie between you and the target (Figure 3-20).

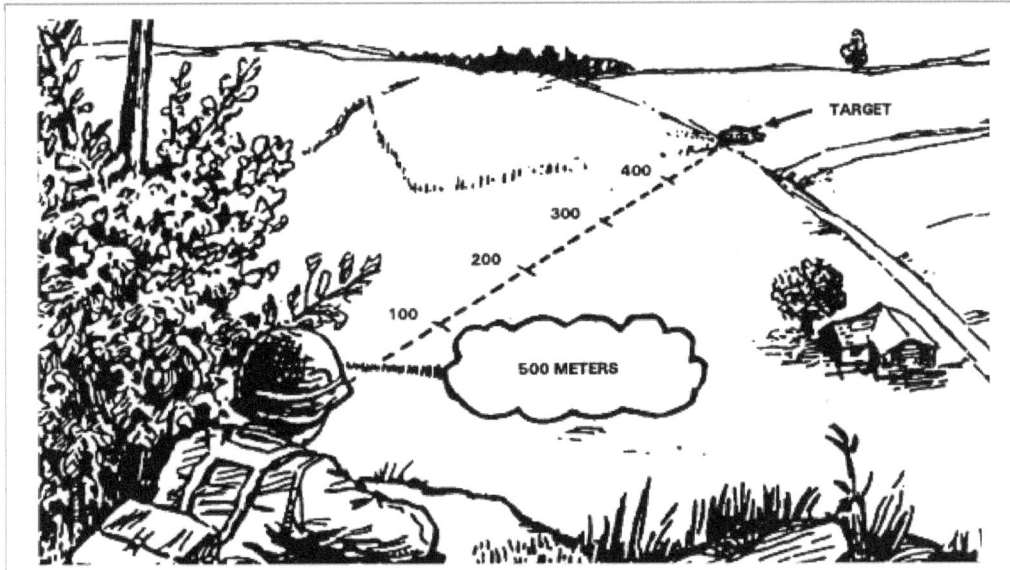

Figure 3-20 Application of the 100-meter unit-of-measurement method

TYPES OF TARGETS

Targets for operators in combat are most likely to be enemy troops. Personnel targets have width and depth; different troop formations require different classes of fire distribution. The fire must thoroughly cover the area where the enemy is known or suspected to be, and the targets may be easy or hard to find.

1. **Point Targets-** These are targets--such as enemy bunkers, windows, weapons emplacements, light-skinned vehicles, and troops--that have a single aiming point. The maximum effective range for point targets is 150 meters.

2. **Area Targets-** These may have considerable width and depth and may require extensive right or left and searching fire. A deployed platoon is one example of an area target. The operator must know how to engage area targets regardless of their sizes or shapes. The maximum effective range for area targets is 350 meters. Types of area targets are as follows:

   A. **Linear Targets-** The operator sights on what appears to be center of mass. He fires the grenade launcher left and right across the target on successive aiming points.

   B. **Deep Targets-** The operator first lays on the center of mass of the target. He fires searching fire to the near end and then up to the far end of the target along successive aiming points.

   C. **Linear Targets with Depth-** The operator lays on the target's center of mass. He then moves the grenade launcher left and right across the target, selecting successive aiming points at different ranges (FigureA-34).

Section 4

Performance Problems

Malfunction and Immediate Action Procedures

A malfunction occurs when a mechanical failure prevents the weapon from firing properly. Neither defective ammunition nor improper operation of the weapon by the firer is a malfunction. The weapon should be cleaned, lubricated, and retried. If it still fails to function, it should be turned in to the unit armorer. Malfunctions are usually preventable through good practices, but they may still occur out of the blue from time to time. Of course, you hope it is on the practice range, but you should treat each one as though you are in a life-or-death situation. Practicing proper and effective corrective actions will allow you to be more confident in your grenade launcher handling. In stressful situations, you can become much more stressed due to an unforeseen malfunction that is easy to correct.

A stoppage is an unintentional interruption in the cycle of operation or functioning that may be cleared by immediate action. A stoppage is classified by its relationship to the cycle of functioning.

Malfunction drills must fix the problem 100% of the time (excluding a weapon stoppage—broken weapon) the first time performed. You must look at the grenade launcher and identify the problem (obviously the grenade launcher is not functioning as you need, so you must transition to another weapon or rectify the situation). It is a non-functioning weapon at this point—fix it.

You should always practice taking a covered position to correct malfunctions with considerations on how you operate.

The following pages in this chapter describe and detail corrective actions for the various malfunctions that may be encountered.

MALFUNCTIONS

1. FAILURE TO COCK:

Probable Cause	**Corrective Action**
A. Broken Sear	Turn in for armorer maintenance.
B. Improper assembly of cocking lever	Turn in for armorer maintenance.
C. Loose, broken, or missing cocking-lever spring pin	Turn in for armorer maintenance.

STOPPAGES

1. FAILURE TO FIRE:

Probable Cause	**Corrective Action**
A. Safety ON (safety in rear)	Place in FIRE position.
B. Empty chamber	Load.
C. Faulty ammunition	Reload.
D. Water or excess lubricant in firing pin well	Hand cycle weapon several times to include pulling the trigger.
E. Worn or broken firing pin	Turn in for armorer maintenance.
F. Dirt or residue in firing-pin recess	Clean.
G. Weak or broken firing-pin spring	Turn in for armorer maintenance.

2. FAILURE TO EXTRACT:

Probable Cause	**Corrective Action**
A. Defective extractor spring or spring pin ruptured cartridge case	Turn in for armorer maintenance.

3. FAILURE TO EJECT:

Probable Cause	**Corrective Action**
A. Worn, broken, or missing ejector spring or retainer	Turn in for armorer maintenance.

4. FAILURE TO CHAMBER:

Probable Cause	**Corrective Action**
A. Faulty ammunition	Reload.
B. Dirty chamber	Clean bore and chamber.

5. SAFETY FAILS TO STAY IN POSITION:

Probable Cause	**Corrective Action**
A. Missing spring pin or broken or worn safety	Turn in for armorer maintenance.

IMMEDIATE ACTION PROCEDURES

Immediate action refers to anything an operator does to reduce a stoppage without taking time to look for the cause. Immediate action should be taken in the event of either a hangfire or misfire. Either can be caused by an ammunition defect or by a faulty firing mechanism. Any failure to fire must be considered a hangfire until that possibility is eliminated.

- A <u>hangfire</u> is a delay in the functioning of the round's propelling-charge explosive train at the time of firing. The length of this delay is unpredictable, but in most cases, it ranges between a split second and 30 seconds. Such a delay in the functioning of the round could result from the presence of excess oil or grease, grit, sand, frost, or ice.

- A <u>misfire</u> is a complete failure of the weapon to fire. A misfire in itself is not dangerous, but because it cannot be immediately distinguished from a hangfire, it must be considered to be a hangfire until proven otherwise.

Because a stoppage may be caused by a hangfire, the following precautions must be observed until the round has been removed from the weapon and the cause of the failure determined:

- Keep the M79 pointed downrange or at the target and keep everyone clear of its muzzle. If the stoppage occurs during training, shout MISFIRE and clear the area of any operators not needed for the operation.
- Wait 30 seconds from the time of the failure before opening the barrel assembly to perform the unloading procedure.
- After removing the round from the receiver, determine whether the round or the firing mechanism is defective. Examine the primer to see if it is dented. If the primer is dented, separate the round from other ammunition until it can be disposed of properly. However, if the primer is not dented, the firing mechanism is at fault. Once the cause of the failure to fire has been corrected, the round may be reloaded and fired.

WARNING- If you are unloading a weapon that has not been fired, avoid detonation either by catching the ejected round or by holding the weapon close to the ground to reduce the distance the round can fall.

REMEDIAL ACTION PROCEDURES

Remedial action is any action taken by the gunner to restore his weapon to operational condition. Take remedial action only if immediate action does not remedy the problem.

DESTRUCTION PROCEDURES

Destruction of any military weapon is necessary as a last resort to prevent the enemy from capturing or using it. This paragraph discusses planning for destruction, priorities and methods of destruction, and degree of damage. In combat situations, the commander has the authority to destroy weapons, but he must report doing so through channels.

1. **Planning-** SOPs for all teams should contain a plan for destroying equipment. Having such a plan ensures that the damage is effective enough to deny use of the equipment to the enemy. The plan must be flexible enough in its designation of time, equipment, and personnel to meet any situation.

2. **Priorities of Destruction-** When lack of time prevents them from completely destroying equipment, operators must destroy the same essential parts on all like equipment. The order in which the parts should be destroyed (priority of destruction) is as follows:
    A. Breech mechanism.
    B. Barrel.
    C. Sights or sighting equipment.

3. **Methods of Destruction-** Equipment may be destroyed by any of several methods. The commander must use his imagination and resourcefulness to select the best method of destruction based on the facilities available. Time is usually critical. The methods of destruction are as follows:
    A. **Mechanical-** Use an axe, pick, sledgehammer, crowbar, or other heavy implement.
    B. **Burning-** Use gasoline, oil, incendiary grenades, other flammables, or a welding or cutting torch.
    C. **Demolition-** Use suitable explosives or ammunition or, as a last resort, hand grenades.
    D. **Disposal-** Bury essential parts, dump them in streams, or scatter them so widely that recovering them would be impossible.

4. **Degree of Damage**- The method of destruction used must damage equipment and essential spare parts to the extent that they cannot be restored to usable condition in the combat zone, either by repair or by cannibalization.

Appendix A - Ammunition

Types, Characteristics and Capabilities of Ammunition used with the M79 Grenade Launcher.

The most commonly used ammunition for the M79 is the M406 antipersonnel round, which has a lethal radius of five meters, and the M433 multi-purpose round which, in addition to having fragmentation effects, will penetrate up to 3 inches (7.6 cm) of armor plate. Many other types of ammunition are available, such as buckshot, tear gas, and various signal rounds, which greatly increase the versatility of this outstanding weapon.

The M406 40mm HE grenades fired from the M79 traveled at a muzzle velocity of 75 meters per second, and contained enough explosive within a steel casing that, upon impact with the target, would produce over 300 fragments at 1,524 meters per second within a lethal radius of up to 5 meters. Stabilized in flight by the spin imparted on it by the rifled barrel, the grenade rotated at 3,700 rpm; this in turn, after approximately 15 meters of flight, armed the grenade.

WARNING
- The 40mm grenades used in the M79 (40x46mm) are not the same as in the Mk 19 grenade launcher (40x53mm), which are fired at a higher velocity.
- All issued grenades must be inspected for faults- dents and cracks.
- Do not fire ammunition not made for use In the M79 grenade launcher. Doing so will result in injury to, or death of, personnel.
- If fired into snow or mud, 40-mm rounds may not hit hard enough to detonate. An undetonated round may explode when stepped on or driven over. During training in snow or mud, avoid this hazard by firing only TP rounds.
- If ammunition fails to fire in your weapon, turn it in to unit armorer for disposition.
- Do not fire Pyrotechnic Ammunition made for the AN-M8 pyrotechnic pistol in the M79 Grenade Launcher. It is very dangerous.
- Make sure you have the right ammunition!
- Never load aircraft ammunition M384 (HE) or M385 (practice). You may blow your head off.

Packaging

Typically HE, HEDP, and TP are shipped in wooden boxes containing two metal ammo cans, with three bandoleers of six rounds each, for a total of 18 rounds per metal ammo, and 36 rounds per wooden box.

Combat Load

The recommended minimum combat load is 18 rounds of the 40mm ammunition.

Figure A-1 Various cartridges available for the M79

Cartridges for the M203 grenade launcher

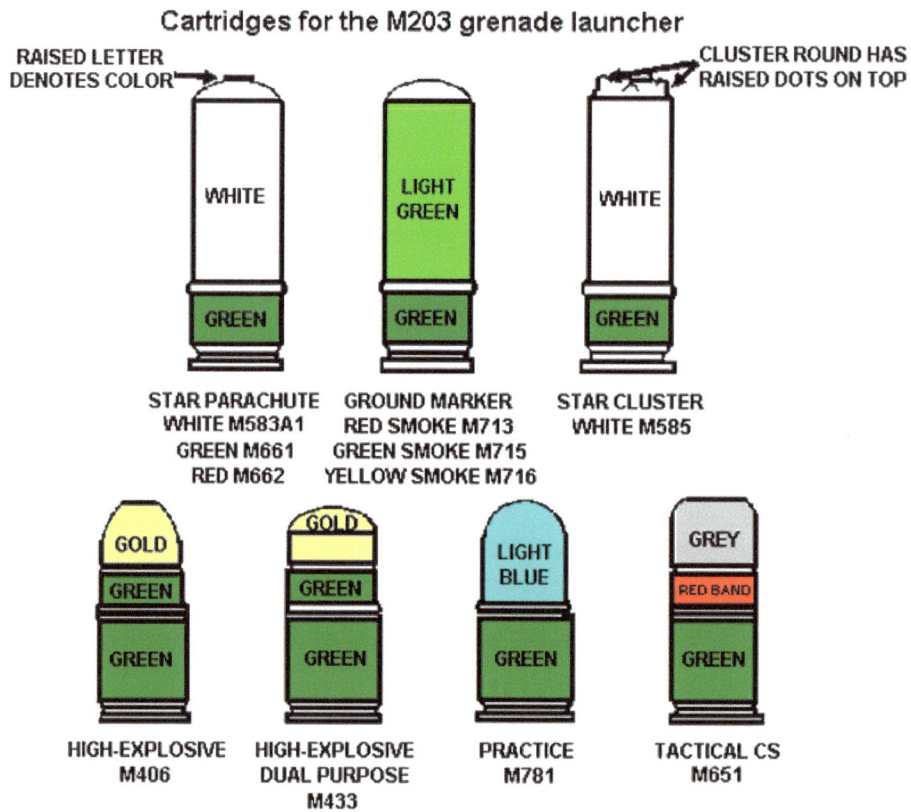

RAISED LETTER
DENOTES COLOR

CLUSTER ROUND HAS
RAISED DOTS ON TOP

WHITE	LIGHT GREEN	WHITE
GREEN	GREEN	GREEN

STAR PARACHUTE
WHITE M583A1
GREEN M661
RED M662

GROUND MARKER
RED SMOKE M713
GREEN SMOKE M715
YELLOW SMOKE M716

STAR CLUSTER
WHITE M585

GOLD	GOLD	LIGHT BLUE	GREY
GREEN	GREEN		RED BAND
GREEN	GREEN	GREEN	GREEN

HIGH-EXPLOSIVE
M406

HIGH-EXPLOSIVE
DUAL PURPOSE
M433

PRACTICE
M781

TACTICAL CS
M651

Figure A-2 Various cartridges available for the M79

High-explosive Dual-purpose Round, M433. The HEDP round has an olive drab aluminum skirt with a steel cup attached, white markings, and a gold ogive (head of the round). It penetrates at least 5 cm (2 inches) when fired straight at steel armor at 150 meters or less, or at a point target, it arms between 14 and 27 meters, causes casualties within a 130-meter radius, and has a kill radius of 5 meters.

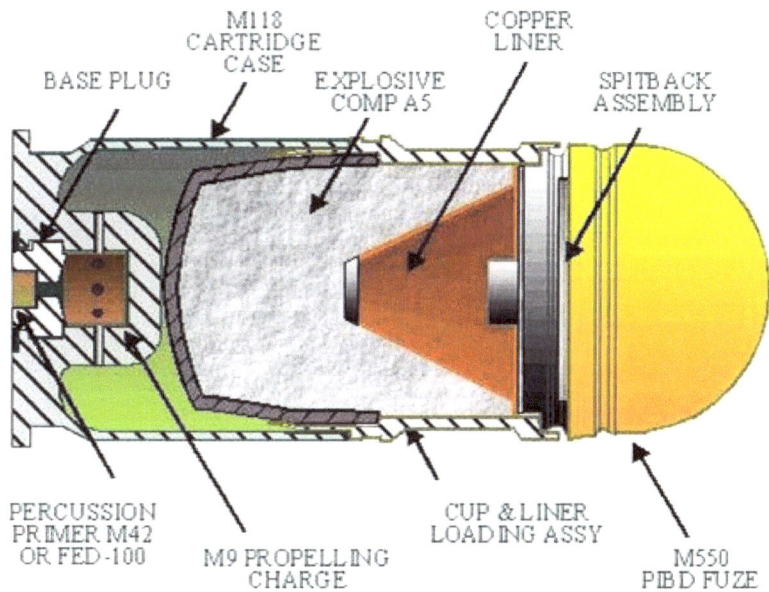

40mm M433 High Explosive Dual Purpose Cartridge

HEDP ROUND, M433
DODAC 1310-B546

LENGTH
10.29 CM (4.05 IN)

WEIGHT
0.23 KG (0.51 LB)

Figures A-3 M33 HEDP

High-explosive Round, M406. The HE round has an olive drab aluminum skirt with a steel projectile attached, gold markings, and a yellow ogive. It arms between 14 and 27 meters, produces a ground burst that causes casualties within a 130-meter radius, and has a kill radius of 5 meters.

HE ROUND, M406
DODAC 1310-B566

LENGTH
9.89 CM (3.89 IN)

WEIGHT
0.23 KG (0.51 LB)

Figure A-4 M406 HE

40MM AMMUNITION PYROTECHNIC SIGNAL AND SPOTTING ROUNDS

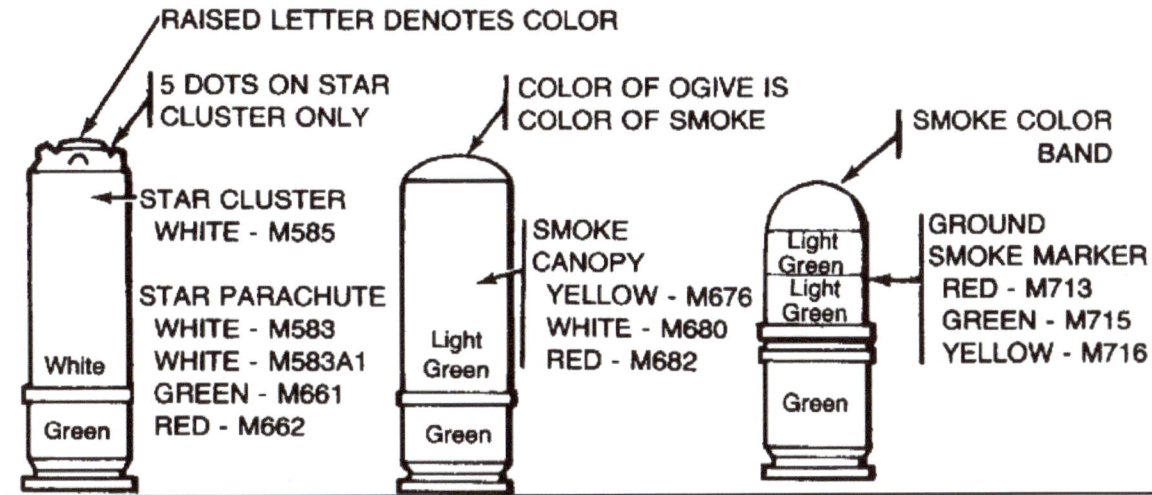

RAISED LETTER DENOTES COLOR

5 DOTS ON STAR
CLUSTER ONLY

STAR CLUSTER
WHITE - M585

STAR PARACHUTE
WHITE - M583
WHITE - M583A1
GREEN - M661
RED - M662

White
Green

COLOR OF OGIVE IS
COLOR OF SMOKE

SMOKE
CANOPY
YELLOW - M676
WHITE - M680
RED - M682

Light
Green

Green

SMOKE COLOR
BAND

Light
Green
Light
Green

Green

GROUND
SMOKE MARKER
RED - M713
GREEN - M715
YELLOW - M716

Figure A-5 Pyrotechnic signal

White Star Cluster Round, M585. This round is white-impact or bar-aluminum alloy with black markings. The attached plastic ogive has five raised dots for night identification. The round is used for illumination or signals. It is lighter and more accurate than comparable handheld signal rounds. The individual stars burn for about 7 seconds during free fall.

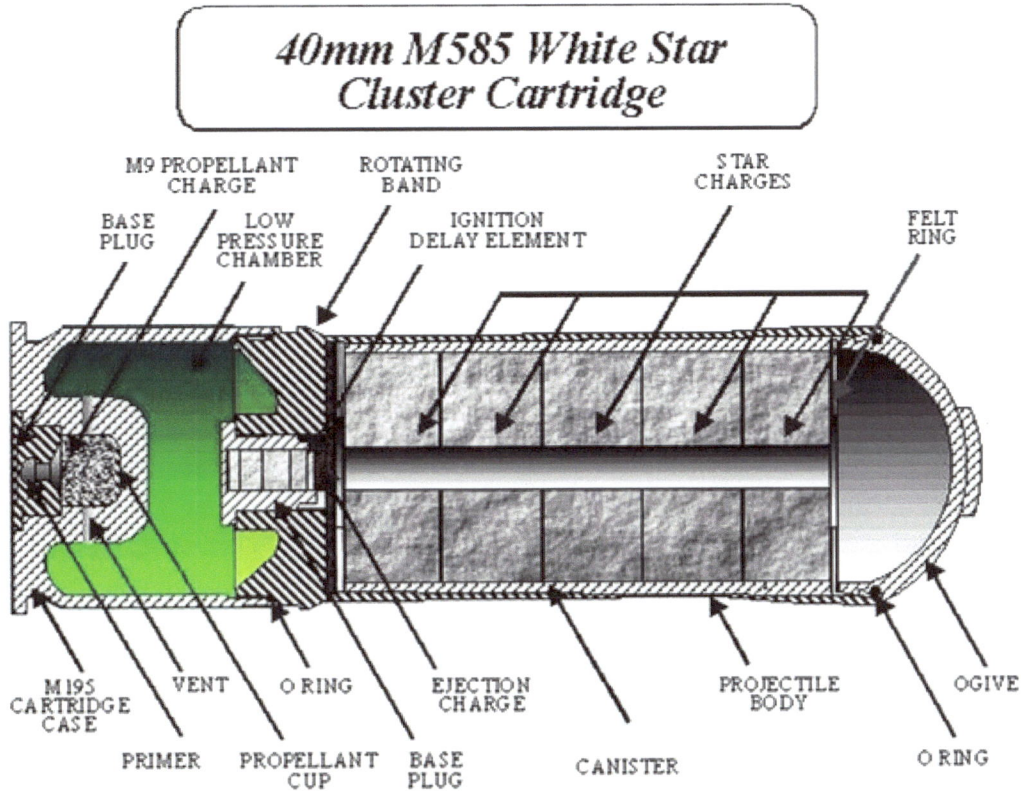

40mm M585 White Star Cluster Cartridge

M9 PROPELLANT CHARGE
ROTATING BAND
STAR CHARGES
BASE PLUG
LOW PRESSURE CHAMBER
IGNITION DELAY ELEMENT
FELT RING
M195 CARTRIDGE CASE
VENT
O RING
EJECTION CHARGE
PROJECTILE BODY
OGIVE
PRIMER
PROPELLANT CUP
BASE PLUG
CANISTER
O RING

Figure A-6 M585 White Star Cluster, cutaway

STAR CLUSTER ROUND

WHITE, M585
    DODAC 1310-B536

LENGTH
    13.38 CM (5.27 IN)

WEIGHT
    0.19 KG (0.41 LB)

Figure A-7 M585 White Star Cluster

Star Parachute Round- M583A1 (White), M661 (Green), M662 (Red), XM992 (Infrared). This round is white-impact or bar-alloy aluminum with black markings. It is used for illumination and signals and is lighter and more accurate than comparable handheld signal rounds. The parachute attached to the round deploys upon ejection to lower the candle at 7 feet per second. The candle burns for about 40 seconds. A raised letter on the top of the round denotes the color of the parachute.

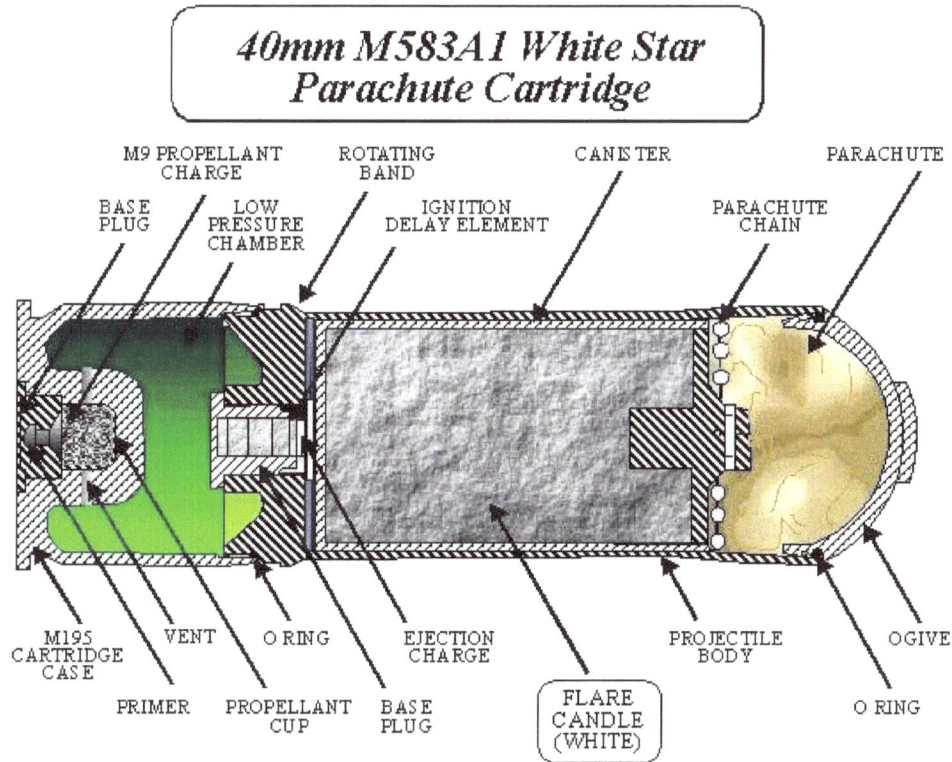

Figure A-8 M583A1 White Star Cluster, cutaway

STAR PARACHUTE ROUNDS

WHITE, M583A1
  DODAC 1310-B534
  90,000 CANDLEPOWER

GREEN, M661
  DODAC 1310-B504
  8,000 CANDLEPOWER

RED, M662
  DODAC 1310-B505
  20,000 CANDLEPOWER

LENGTH
  13.39 CM (5.27 IN)

WEIGHT
  0.22 KG (0.49 LB)

Figure A-9 Star Parachute

Ground Marker Round- M713 (Red), M715 (Green), M716 (Yellow). This round is light-green impact aluminum with black markings. The color of the ogive indicates the color of the smoke.

The round is not for screening. It is used for aerial identification and for marking the location of soldiers on the ground. If a fuze fails to function on impact, the output mixture provided in the front end of the delay casing backs up the impact feature.

GROUND MARKER (SMOKE) ROUNDS

RED, M713
  DODAC 1310-B506

GREEN, M715
  DODAC 1310-B508

YELLOW, M716
  DODAC 1310-B509

LENGTH
  9.93 CM (3.91 IN)

WEIGHT
  0.22 KG (0.49 LB)

LIGHT GREEN

GREEN

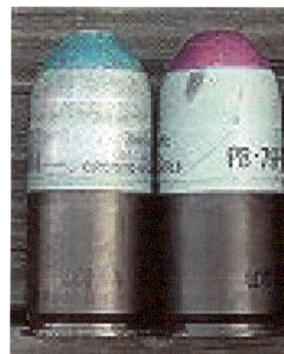

Figure A-10 Smoke

The round consists of a cartridge case, a projectile with pyrotechnic smoke payload, and a pyrotechnic impact fuze.

1. The **cartridge case** is a dual-chambered aluminum container housing a brass propellant cup. The propellant cup is held in the case by a crimped base plug which provides a pressure-type waterproof seal.
2. The **projectile** utilizes a one-piece, aluminum body-ogive and a steel base. The payload consists of a pyrotechnic smoke mixture pressed into the body ogive with a cylindrical cavity in the center.
3. The **fuze** is cemented to the base of the projectile and protrudes into cylindrical cavity of the smoke mixture.

The muzzle velocity is expected to be approximately 254 fps (77 mps), and the maximum range is 437 yards (400 m).

Operation:
1. Upon firing, the primer ignites the propellant charge. In addition to launching the projectile, propellant gases ignite the first-fire mixture of the fuze in base

of the projectile. The first-fire mixture ignites a high-temperature transfer mixture contained in the steel cup. The transfer mixture burns during the first 15 meters of projectile flight.

2. When the projectile is between 15 and 45 meters from the launcher muzzle, heat transfer through the steel cup ignites the delay mixture.

3. Upon impact, the delay casing breaks and the burning portion flies forward out of the fuze support, contacting and igniting the pyrotechnic smoke mixture.

4. Ignition of the smoke mixture causes a buildup of pressure that dislodges the fuze support at the aft end of the projectile, thus allowing smoke to be emitted at the aft end of the projectile.

5. Projectile impact prior to the minimum arming distance (15 meters) results in a dud. Between 15 and 45 meters from the launcher muzzle, the fuze may or may not function upon impact.

6. In the event that the fuze fails to function upon impact, the output mixture provided in the front end of the delay casing acts as a backup to the impact feature. When the flame reaches this point (8 to 10 seconds after launch), the output mixture flashes and ignites the smoke mixture.

Thermobaric Grenade, XM1060
The XM1060 40mm Thermobaric Grenade, developed and fielded by Picatinny Arsenal within a four-month span, is the very first small arms thermobaric device released to a US war theatre. It is applauded as a critical tool for military operations in urban terrain and close-quarters cave applications.

Thermobaric cartridges provide operators with a significantly greater probability of kill/incapacitation within the effective radius. The lethality effect results from a thermobaric overpressure blast rather than fragmentation. As a result of the thermobaric reaction, all enemy personnel within the effective radius will suffer lethal effects as opposed to the conventional fragmentation round.

In order to meet the short deadline, it was decided to use existing 40mm ammunition components. The 40mm 550 fuze, the M195 cartridge case, and a modified version of the M583 projectile body were used along with an YJ-05 thermobaric mix (a proprietary mix from contractor Ensign Bickford).

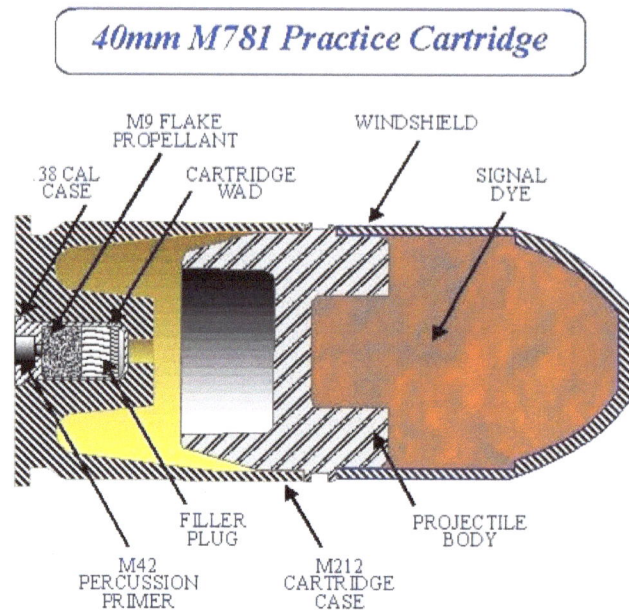

Figure A-11 M781 Practice, cutaway

Practice Round, M781. Used for practice, this round is blue zinc or aluminum with white markings. It produces a yellow or orange signature on impact, arms between 14 and 27 meters, and has a danger radius of 20 meters. The M781 is a low-cost, unfuzed, fixed-round of practice ammunition ready for use as issued. The cartridge case is made of plastic material and the projectile is also plastic with an aluminum-rotating band. The ogive is made of a frangible plastic material and contains a colored dye in granular form, the consistency of talcum powder, which is used to generate a signature. The propulsion system consists of a standard .38 caliber blank.

PRACTICE ROUND, M781
DODAC 1310-B518

LENGTH
10.29 CM (4.05 IN)

WEIGHT
0.22 KG (0.48 LB)

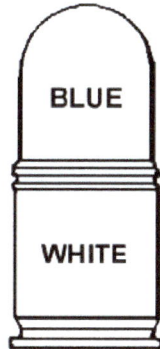

Figure A-12

Training/Practice (TP) Round, M918. Used for practice, this round is blue zinc or aluminum with white markings. It produces a yellow or orange signature on impact, arms between 14 and 27 meters, and has a danger radius of 20 meters.

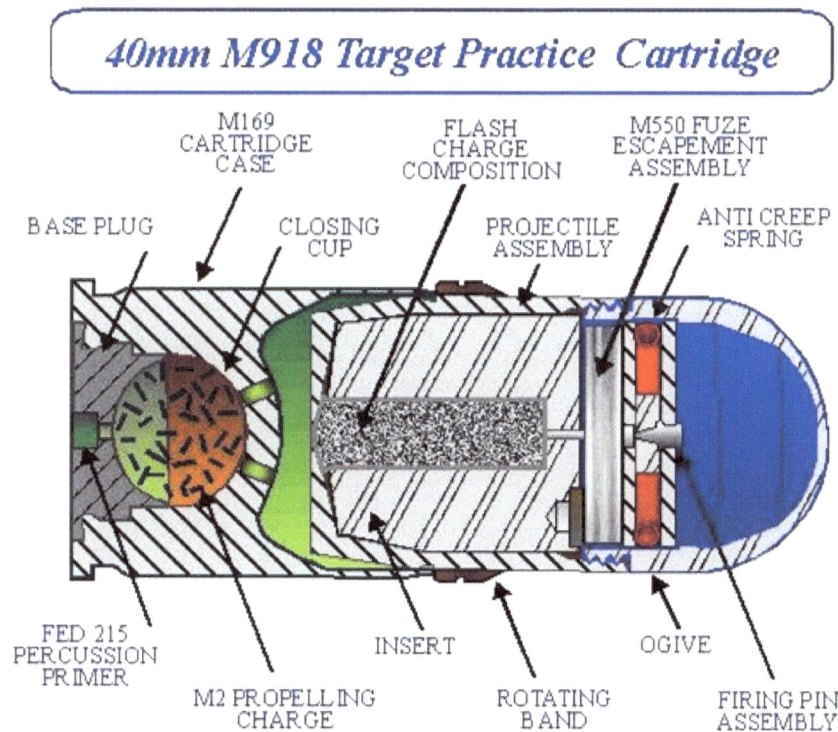

Figure A-13 M918 Target/Practice, cutaway

CS Round, M651. This round is gray aluminum with a green casing and black markings. Though it is a multipurpose round, it is most effective for riot control and in Military Operations in Urban Terrain (MOUT). It arms between 10 and 30 meters and produces a white cloud of CS gas on impact.

TACTICAL CS ROUND, M651
DODAC 1310-B567

LENGTH
11.43 CM (4.50 IN)

WEIGHT
0.22 KG (0.48 LB)

GREY

RED BAND

GREEN

Figure A-14 M651 Tactical CS

The round is filled with about 2 ounces (57 g) of CS pyrotechnic mix containing approximately 0.75 ounces (21 g) of CS. Maximum accuracy is obtained at ranges up to 219 yards (200 m). Area targets may be engaged up to 437 yards (400 m). This projectile can penetrate window glass or up to 3/4 inch-thick pine at 200 meters and still release CS. Following impact, a cloud of CS is emitted for approximately 25 seconds. Area coverage: approximately 144 square yards (120 square meters). Two cartridges effectively placed will incapacitate 95% of unmasked personnel in an enclosure of 15 by 30 by 20 feet within 60 seconds after functioning.

Buckshot Round, M576. This round is olive drab with black markings. For close-range fighting, the Army came up with two types of M79 rounds. The first was a flechette round (or Bee Hives round) which housed approx 45 small darts in a plastic casing; these rounds were issued on an experimental basis. Later this round was replaced by the M-576 buckshot round. This round contained 27- 00 buckshot, which on firing was carried down the barrel in a 40mm plastic sabot which slowed down in flight so that the pellets could travel in their forward direction unaided.

Though it is a multipurpose round, it is most effective in thickly vegetated areas or for room clearing. Inside it has at least 2,000 pellets, which cast a cone of fire 30 meters wide and 30 meters high and travel at 269 meters per second. Be sure to aim buckshot rounds at the foot of the target. The round has no mechanical-type fuse. Photo shows them in the molded plastic carry case.

Figure A-15 M576 Buckshot

Non-lethal Round, M1006. This round incapacitates a targeted individual with Non-lethal blunt trauma from 15-30 meters and provides a non-lethal means of crowd control. The non-lethal 40mm cartridge provides friendly forces with the capability to stop, confuse, disorient, or momentarily deter a potential threat without using deadly force. Military forces use this non-lethal cartridge to apply the minimum force necessary while performing missions of crowd control and site and area security of key facilities throughout the world. The non-lethal 40mm cartridge is intended to be a direct fire, low-hazard, non-shrapnel-producing device which will produce less than lethal trauma upon impact.

The 40mm-sponge grenade provides temporary incapacitation through blunt trauma. It provides a tactical alternative for dealing with low-intensity conflicts, peacekeeping missions, and humanitarian relief missions. The projectile consists of a foam rubber nose and a high-density plastic projectile body fired from the 40mm M203 or M79 Grenade Launchers. Minimum engagement range is 10 - 15 meters, and maximum effective range is 50 meters. Velocity at 50 meters is 200 feet per second. Also available are reload kits. Each kit consists of shell cases, rotating bands, and foam ogives in quantities of 48-, 72-, 96- and 120- shot quantities. These kits are for training purpose only.

Available from **www.vig-sec.com**

Muzzle Velocity- 76 m/s (250 f/s)
Effective Range- 27.4 m (30 yards)
Projectile Weight- 60 gm (1.192 oz)
Overall Weight- 100 g (3.5 oz)

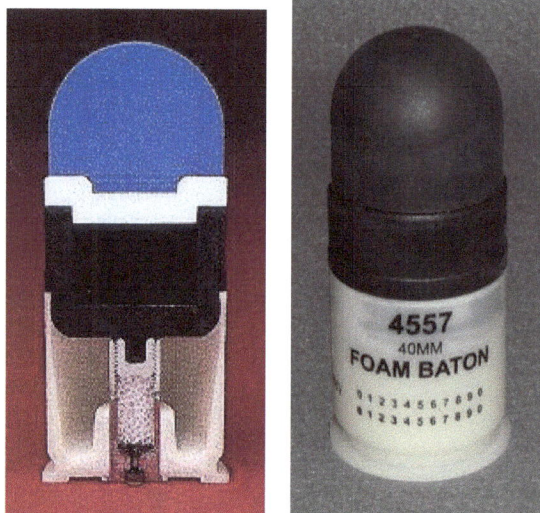

Figures A-16 BH-CTS-4557

CTS Sting Ball Cartridge [Like a Crowd Dispersal Round (Area), M1029]

The 40mm Sting Ball™ rubber-pellet cartridge is designed to be skip fired in situations where collateral damage and serious injury to innocent bystanders is to be avoided. All our cartridge cases are made of aluminum alloy. These cartridges were developed specifically for 40mm grenade launchers such as the U.S. M203, M79, and the CTS TGL-1. The cartridge case fully chambers in such launchers, eliminating the possibility of the cartridge slipping past the extractor, as may occur with undersized cartridges. The undercut at the cartridge base further ensures reliable extraction after every shot. Available in .31 or .60 caliber sting balls.

The Less Lethal Crowd Dispersal Cartridge is a direct-fire, low-hazard, non-shrapnel-producing projectile 40mm non-lethal cartridge effective for crowd dispersions or routing of individuals in crowd control or civil disturbance situations and against subjects who offer violent resistance. The round is extremely effective against individuals in a violent mindset or armed with impact or edged weapons. It is also effective against rioters and in rescue or street-clearing operations. **Available from www.vig-sec.com**

BH-CTS-4553 (.31 Caliber Balls)   **BH-CTS-4558 (.60 caliber balls)**

Although non-lethal ammunition is designed to help control a hostile individual or crowd without serious injury or death to targeted individuals, such instances may still occur even when non-lethal munitions are properly employed. Engaging targets at less than 10 meters greatly increases the potential lethality of this munition.

The payload spreads out from the barrel to cover an area equal to five standard E-type silhouettes standing side by side at a range of 30 meters. Be aware of possible bounce-back if fired at a wall or hard object within 20 meters of the user.

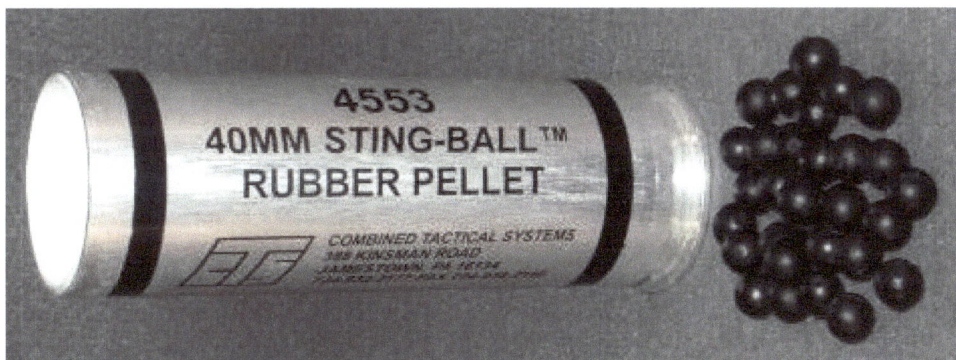

Figure A-17

40mm Kinetic Less-Lethal Rounds

CTS manufactures a complete line of 40mm less-lethal impact munitions, cartridges with rubber foam or hardwood batons. All our cartridge cases are made of aluminum alloy. Wood batons are coated and sealed with lacquer to prevent swelling through moisture absorption. These cartridges were developed specifically for 40mm grenade launchers such as the U.S. M203, M79, and the CTS TGL-1. The cartridge case fully chambers in such launchers, eliminating the possibility of the cartridge slipping past the extractor, as may occur with undersized cartridges. The undercut at the cartridge base further ensures reliable extraction after every shot. **Available from www.vig-sec.com**

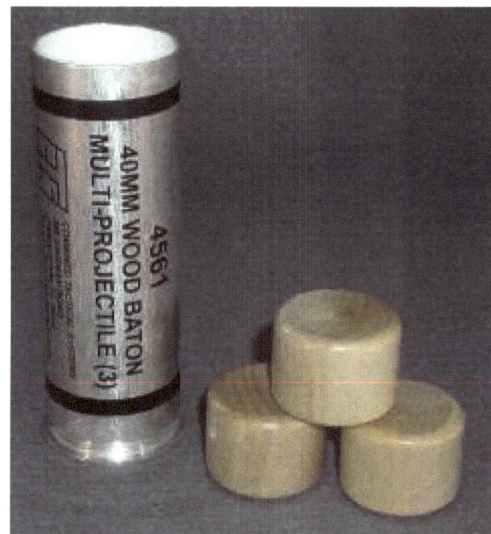

BH-CTS-4551 (Foam Baton)   **BH-CTS-4561 (Wood Baton)**
Figure A-18 CTS Baton Projectiles

40mm Liquid & Powder Barricade Projectiles

Developed specifically for rifled grenade launchers such as the U.S. M79 and the TGL-1, these cartridges shoot projectiles that engage the barrel rifling. As a result, the projectiles are spin stabilized and therefore highly accurate. The propelling system is based on the one used in the U.S. M781 40mm practice round and uses an M212 high- and low-pressure chamber cartridge case. This proven design keeps reliability high and costs low. The round is available in CN tear agent, CS riot control agent, OC, and inert for training purposes in the liquid munitions, and CS, OC, and inert in the powder munitions. Since no fins are required for stabilization, the total of the projectile length can be used to contain agent.

The impact during target penetration ruptures a weakened circular section in the projectile nose, releasing the payload. The violent deceleration coupled with the spin instantly produce a large volume of either aerosol mist or a fine powder inside the target. **Available from www.vig-sec.com**

Effective Range- 45 m (50 yards)
Muzzle Velocity- 122 m/s (400 f/s)
Overall Weight- 150 gm (5.3 oz)
Overall Height- 122 mm (4.8 inches)

Available in-
BH-CTS-4300 Inert Liquid Barricade **BH-CTS-4401 Inert Powder Barricade**
BH-CTS-4320 CN Liquid Barricade **BH-CTS-4431 CS Powder Barricade**
BH-CTS-4330 CS Liquid Barricade **BH-CTS-4441 OC Powder Barricade**
BH-CTS-4340 OC Liquid Barricade

Figure A-19

40mm Pyrotechnic Smoke Cartridge

These cartridges were developed specifically for 40mm grenade launchers such as the U.S. M79 and the TGL-1. The cartridge case fully chambers in such launchers, eliminating the possibility of the cartridge slipping past the extractor, as may occur with undersized cartridges. The undercut at the cartridge base further ensures reliable extraction after every shot. These rounds are available in CN tear agent, CS riot control agent, and white smoke for screening and tactical purposes. Smoke is emitted from ports at both ends of the projectile. **Available from www.vig-sec.com**

Effective Range- 100 m (110 yds)
Overall Weight- 235 gm (8.3 oz)
Overall Length- 122 mm (4.8 inches)

Available in-
BH-CTS-4210 Inert Smoke
BH-CTS-4220 CN Smoke
BH-CTS-4230 CS Smoke

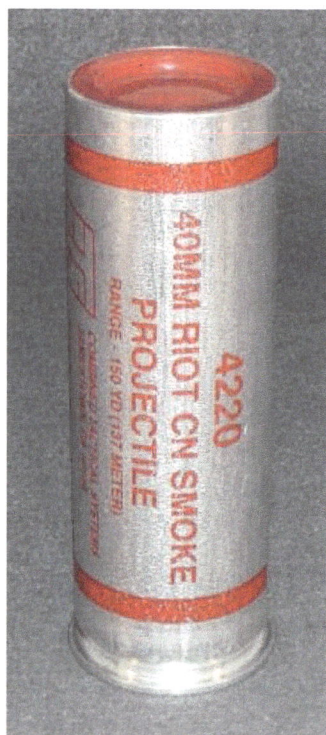

Figure A-20 BH-CTS-4220

40mm Spin-Stabilized Flash-Bang Projectile

The Model 4090 is designed for use in 40mm rifled launchers such as the M203, M79, and the TGL-1. The round uses the proven M212 cartridge case for propulsion. The flash-charge payload is contained in a rubber and plastic projectile, which is spin stabilized for accuracy. The flash charge is initiated by a pyrotechnic delay. Dual in-line delays are used for safety.

This round provides a loud report and a bright flash 328 meters downrange. The resulting rubber and plastic fragments are low in kinetic energy and present a low risk of injury. Ballistic and timing accuracy enable precise placement of single shots or multiple shot patterns. This round is especially effective when used in conjunction with the CTS TGL-6 six-shot rotary magazine launcher.
Available from www.vig-sec.com

Effective Range- 300 m (330 yds)
Sound Output- 175 db @ 1.52 m (5 feet)
Light Output- 6-8 million candelas, 8.5 milliseconds
Overall Weight- 120 gm (6.9 oz)
Overall Length- 122 mm (4.8 inches)

Available in-
BH-CTS-4090

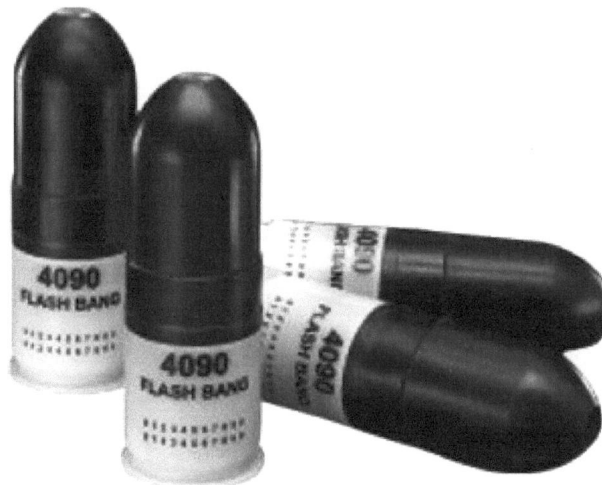

Figure A-21 BH-CTS-4090

HELLHOUND (High Order Unbelievably Nasty Destructive Series) 40MM LV Multi-purpose Grenade

The **HELLHOUND** 40mm Low-velocity Multi-purpose Grenade is a fixed-type ammunition designed to be fired from a 40mm grenade launcher such as the M79, M203 (attached to the M16/M16A1/M16A2 rifle), or Milkor MGL-140. The round consists of an A5-filled metal projectile body with a rotating band, a point-initiating base-detonating fuze with Safe and Arm technology, and a cartridge-case assembly. Upon impact with the target, the firing pin is driven into the detonator, which in turn initiates the spit-back charge, producing a jet which initiates the explosive train from the base forward, resulting in an armor-piercing jet of molten metal and fragmentation of the projectile body. With twice the fill amount of an M433, a 40% increase in the shrapnel pattern, and a casualty radius out to **10 meters**, the **HELLHOUND** provides superior performance against both troops in the open and MOUT-type engagements and **unsurpassed door-breaching capabilities! Available from www.vig-sec.com**

Figure A-22 Hellhound

HELLHOUND

Technical Information
Type- HEDP
Fuze- SF801/M550
Charge- A5
Body Material- Steel
Weight- 225 grams (98 grams A5)
Length- 110 mm
Weapons- M79, M203, Milkor MGL-140 launchers
Penetration- 90 mm mild steel at normal impact with antipersonnel fragmentation
Range Max.- 400 m (437.6 yds)
Muzzle Velocity- 80 mps (262 fps)

DRACO (**D**irect **R**ange **A**ir **C**onsuming **O**rdnance)
40MM LV Multi-purpose Grenade

The **DRACO** 40mm Low-velocity Multi-purpose Grenade is a fixed type ammunition designed to be fired from a 40mm grenade launcher such as the M79, M203 (attached to the M16/M16A1/M16A2 rifle), or Milkor MK-1. The round consists of an Enhanced Blast Explosive (EBX)-filled metal projectile body with a rotating band, a point-initiating base-detonating fuze with Safe and Arm technology, and a cartridge case assembly. Upon impact with the target, the firing pin is driven into the detonator, which in turn initiates the spit-back charge, producing a jet which initiates the explosive train from the base forward, resulting in an armor-piercing jet of molten metal and fragmentation of the projectile body. With twice the fill amount of an M433, a 40% larger fragment pattern, and the Thermobaric effect of the EBX compound, the **DRACO** will provide superior performance against both troops in the open and MOUT-type engagements.
Available from www.vig-sec.com

Figure A-23 DRACO

DRACO

Technical Information
Type- Enhanced Blast - Multi-purpose
Fuze- SF801/M550
Charge- EBX
Body Material- Steel
Weight- 225 grams (90 g YJO5)
Length- 120 mm
Weapons- M79, M203, Milkor MK-1 launchers
Penetration- 65 mm mild steel at normal impact with antipersonnel fragmentation
Range Max.- 400 m (437.6 yds)
Muzzle Velocity- 80 mps (262 fps)

www.ingramcontent.com/pod-product-compliance
Lightning Source LLC
Chambersburg PA
CBHW061055090426
42742CB00002B/53